THE SAKHAROV FILE
A Study in Courage

also by Suzanne LeVert

Great Horse Stories

THE SAKHAROV FILE

A Study in Courage

SUZANNE LE VERT

Introduction by
EFREM YANKELEVICH

JULIAN MESSNER ⓂNEW YORK

Published by Julian Messner,
A Division of Simon & Schuster, Inc.
Simon & Schuster Building
Rockefeller Center
1230 Avenue of the Americas
New York, New York 10020

JULIAN MESSNER and colophon are trademarks of Simon & Schuster, Inc.

Manufactured in the United States of America

1 2 3 4 5 6 7 8 9 10

Library of Congress Cataloging-in-Publication Data

LeVert, Suzanne.
   The Sakharov file.

   Bibliography: p.
   Includes index.
   Summary: Introduces the lives of Andrei Sakharov
and his wife, Elena Bonner, against a background of
Russian history, especially since the 1917 Revolution.
Discusses how Dr. Sakharov's and his wife's outspoken
ideas and activities ran afoul of the authorities and ʻ
the punishments they have endured for upholding the
cause of human rights.
   1. Sakharov, Andrei, 1921–   —Juvenile literature.
2. Bonner, Elena—Juvenile literature. 3. Dissenters—
Soviet Union—Biography—Juvenile literature.
[1. Sakharov, Andrei, 1921–   . 2. Bonner, Elena.
3. Dissenters. 4. Physicists. 5. Soviet Union—
History—1917–   ] I. Title.
DK275.S25L48   1986   947.084'092'2 [B] [920] 85-26037
ISBN 0-671-60070-2

Dedicated to the cause of human rights
around the world.

Acknowledgments

I owe an infinite debt of gratitude to François Sauzey, who gave me the inspiration and courage to write this book; to Wendy Barish, for giving me the chance; and to Diane Arico for her patience.

I would also like to thank the following people for their help: Ludmilla Thorne and Barbara Futterman, at Freedom House; Joshua Rubenstein at Amnesty International; Gary Matthews of the U.S. State Department; Dr. Valentin Turchin (for an enlightening and exciting conversation) and most of all, Efrem and Tatyana Yankelevich, for their immense contributions to this book about their family and their country.

And to my wonderful family and friends who have lived through this: You can all uncross your fingers now.

CONTENTS

A Note to the Reader

Andrei Sakharov is a man of great courage and intelligence. His work as a scientist and human rights activist has made him an important international figure. Both through his writings and through those who have come to the United States and spoken of their personal relationships with him in the Soviet Union, we can understand his opinions and, to some extent, his personality as an adult. But because of the nature of the Soviet Union, which you will read about in this book, information about Sakharov as a child is rather limited. His family and friends who now live in the United States knew him only as an adult. Any documents or memoirs that may exist about Sakharov's childhood and youth remain in the Soviet Union. Therefore, unfortunately, parts of this man's life are still hidden from us by the sources of secrecy in the Soviet Union.

It is my hope, however, that the book that follows gives you a picture of a man, and a country, that is interesting and memorable, despite its unavoidable incompleteness.

Andrei Sakharov, in his home in Moscow, approximately 1982. In the bookcase are photographs of his family, including Efrem Yankelevich, his son-in-law; Anya, his granddaughter; on the second shelf, Tatyana, his stepdaughter; and Ruf Bonner, his mother-in-law. The Yankelevichs and Ruf Bonner now live in Newton, Massachusetts. *(Courtesy Efrem Yankelevich)*

Foreword

This book is about the country where I grew up, and about people whom I love and miss very much.

I guess you have heard a lot about the Soviet Union, or Russia, as it is often called. Most of what you have heard is probably true. It is the largest country in the world, occupying most of the Euro-Asian continent. It has great rivers, forests, and plains. It is rather chilly in most parts of Russia, especially in the winter. It is not a free country, and many terrible things have happened there since the revolution in 1917. Yes, it does pose a threat to America and the world. But no, that threat is not all there is to know about the Soviet Union.

I was born in the southwestern part of the Soviet Union, in a country called Ukraine, but spent most of my life in Moscow, the capital of the Soviet Union.

My children, Matvei and Anna, were also born in Russia. Their first words were Russian, but now they go to an American school, in Newton, Massachusetts, and speak fluent English, without an accent.

This book is about their grandfather, Dr. Andrei Dmitrievich Sakharov, who is also my father-in-law. (The middle name is really a *patronymic*, which means that Dr. Sakharov's father's first name was Dmitri. Using a patronymic is the proper way to address an adult in Russia. If your name is John, and your father's name is George, for instance, you would be called John Georgevich in Russia.)

Dr. Sakharov is very famous in many countries, and in Russia too. You might have heard about him on television or in the newspapers. He is famous for two things in his life: he studied physics, and then he defended those who were unjustly persecuted. He also tried to make Russia a little bit more free and a just country, and the world a safer place to live in. He is also a very good and unusual person.

Why is he so famous?

I think people are interested in those who have great talents and have achieved much in their profession. Dr. Sakharov is a very good physicist. He not only invented the thermonuclear bomb for the Soviet government, he also suggested a practical way to use thermonuclear reaction (fusion) to generate heat and electricity. He made important contributions to cosmology (a science about the universe) and to the theory of elementary particles.

But Dr. Sakharov is famous, I think, not just because of the discoveries he made in physics. I think people are interested in him because he encountered in his life certain problems and situations that have important symbolic and practical meanings for our time. He made certain choices and decisions that have affected not only his life, but also the lives of many other people. And people, basically, approve of the choices he made. He is considered to be a "moral authority," and was called by the Nobel Peace Prize Committee, "the conscience of mankind." I think it means that people believe he can tell right from wrong: they believe in his moral judgment.

I saw Dr. Sakharov almost daily for about seven

years, until I had to leave Russia in 1977. I learned much from him and his friends, or at least I would like to think I did.

Most probably you are not going to learn from this book exactly the same things I have learned from Dr. Sakharov, if only because we have very different backgrounds. I am very curious what you, and Matvei and Anna, will learn from this book. And it is not mere curiosity. It is very important for me because, for better or for worse, you will be struggling in your own lives with the problems that today confront Dr. Sakharov, and me, and many other people.

Efrem Yankelevich
May 1985

CHAPTER ONE

Shots Heard Round the World: The Russian Revolution

Gorki is a city located two hundred and fifty miles east of Moscow, in the Soviet Union. It is a place closed to foreigners, and tightly guarded by the KGB, the Soviet secret police. Most of the one million inhabitants of the dark, gray city live much like the rest of Soviet citizenry, but there are a few exceptions. Two of these exceptions are Andrei Dmitrievich Sakharov and his wife, Elena Georgievna Bonner.

It is here in Gorki that they are now forced to live. For more than five years, Dr. Sakharov has been in internal exile—banished from Moscow and forced to live where the authorities tell him. They have told him Gorki. He cannot leave the city or receive any visitors. Elena Bonner had been allowed, under close watch, to travel to Moscow and communicate with friends and relatives until 1984. Then she too was sentenced to internal exile with her husband.

Dr. Bonner had served as a nurse during World War II. She had dedicated herself to the communist cause and the protection of her homeland. Wounded at the front, she rejoined the effort as soon as she was able. When she was discharged, she had achieved the rank of lieutenant in the medical corps.

Dr. Sakharov has an even more impressive background as a servant of the Soviet state. He has, in fact, been at the top of Soviet society. As the "father of the Soviet hydrogen bomb" and a world-renowned scientist, he had bestowed on him the most distinguished honor of the Soviet state, the Hero of Socialist Labor, the highest award in Russia, three times. He was the youngest member ever elected to the USSR Academy of Sciences. Along with these distinctions came the privileges and high salaries of a member of the Soviet elite. At the height of his career, for instance, Dr. Sakharov was earning perhaps five times as much as the average citizen.

Charged with "crimes against the state" and anti-Soviet activity, Drs. Sakharov and Bonner now have no communication with the outside world. They have no telephone. Their apartment is equipped with listening devices placed there by the KGB, and every conversation they have is monitored. They are accompanied by agents whenever they go out to shop, mail letters (which are then confiscated), or simply to take a walk. Neither of them has been seen, by anyone other than the KGB, since April of 1984. (See page 120 for an update.)

What are "crimes against the state?" Who judged them guilty? And why?

To understand the Sakharovs and their fate, it is necessary to take a look at Russian society and the government under which it lives—so different from our own in its form, history, and world view.

It is a fascinating, colossal country. Hedrick Smith, a reporter for *The New York Times,* wrote in his excellent book, *The Russians,* that the average American would have a great deal of trouble imagining "the geographic meaning of a nation that encompasses eleven time zones . . . the fact that Leningrad is much closer to New York than it is to Vladivostok [another *Russian* city!] . . . the United States, plus half of Canada would fit into Siberia [the eastern part of the Soviet Union] *alone.*"

Indeed, Russia is by far the largest country in the world. It has an area of 8,603,006 square miles, over twice that of the United States. The shape of the country is rather oblong, over twice as long stretching east to west than north to south. It has a common border with thirteen countries, with no natural boundaries to separate them. This lack of natural boundaries made Russia the target of a number of invasions from hostile enemies during its early history. Then in World Wars I and II, new, modern armies attacked, leaving the country devastated.

Russia is a country rich with varied and spectacular geography. It has some of the highest mountains, like the volcanic Mount Elbriz (which is 18,481 feet high), and two of the longest rivers, the Yenisei (3,504 miles long) and the Lena (2,562 miles long). A huge desert in Soviet Central Asia, 1,350 miles from east to west and nearly 1,000 miles north to south, is one of the largest in the world.

The climate, by U.S. standards, is preposterous! Throughout nearly all of this enormous country, there are severe winters. Moscow in January, for instance, has an average temperature of 14°F. In eastern Siberia, the temperature is often 50°F—below zero! It never gets very hot, even in the summer, when the average temperature is in the mid-60s. In Central Asia, however, it often will reach as high as 80°F.

One of the most extraordinary features of the Soviet climate exists in the most northern parts. There are periods of up to two months in the winter when the sun never shines, and in the summer when there is no night.

The Russian population is just as vast and diverse as its geography. According to the 1970 census, 250 million people were living in fifteen different republics. The Slavs, including Russians and Ukrainians, make up about half of the population. And ten million more are of non-Slavic origin—Lithuanians, Moldavians, Georgians, Latvians, and Estonians. Then there are the Turkic peoples—the Uzbeks, Tatars, Kazakhs, Turkmen, Kirghiz, and others. Each has a separate identity and distinct history and most have their own language.

There exists in Russia a special group of people—the *intelligentsia*. They are the poets, writers, philosophers, artists, and scientists, and they have been contributing to the grand cultural traditions of their country from the beginning.

Every society has its group of intellectuals, but in

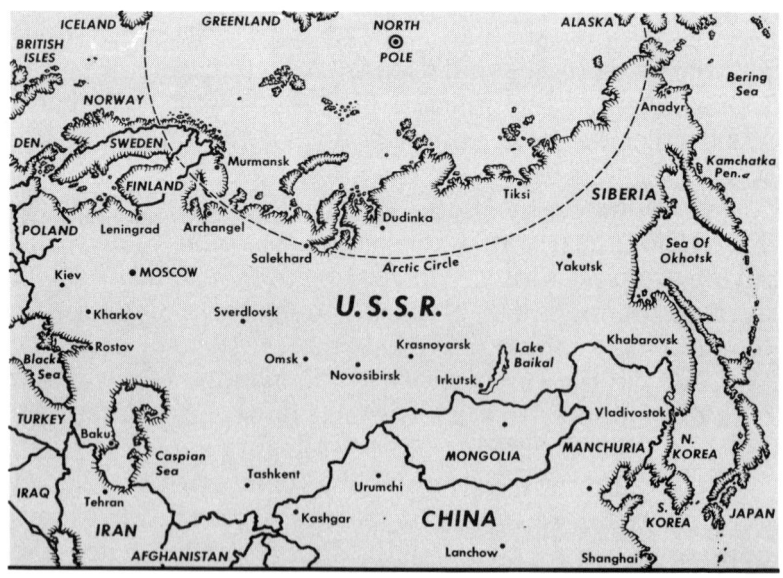

The Soviet Union and surrounding countries. (*Courtesy AP/Wide World Photos*)

Russia, where harsh censorship and restrictions on freedom of speech have long been in effect, this group of people has taken more risks. Taking those risks has given them a special appreciation for the results of their own work, and the work of their predecessors. And more than their work in the arts and sciences, it is their passion for culture, and for a life that centers around ideas rather than only practical day-to-day existence, that distinguishes them from their countrymen. The scarce opportunities to enjoy that kind of life, and the risks that must be taken, are what separates them from their Western counterparts.

The history of Russia is a long and fascinating one. However, the turning point for its people and for the modern world took place merely seventy years ago.

The Russian Revolution

One of the world's greatest upheavals took place during the spring and fall of 1917. It was then that the Russian people, led by a relatively small group of highly educated and dedicated men, rose up against the Tsarist government that had been ruling the country for over a thousand years.

Russia, always a poor and, compared with Western Europe, economically and technologically backward country, was now nearly destitute. It had lost perhaps eight million of its citizens, mostly young men, fighting the Germans at the Russian front in World War I. Nearly 80 percent of its surviving people were peasants, living in one-room thatched-roofed cottages, ekeing out an existence in feudal Tsarist society. The West had already begun its modernization during the Industrial Revolution in the 1800s, but the Russians were far behind.

The educated classes and merchants were materially slightly better off, but even with the formation of the Duma (a constitutional body), were virtually powerless under the Tsar. The royal family and nobility, of course, lived in grand style, for all disgruntled underclasses to see. They were also running an inefficient and corrupt government.

The centuries of feudalism had also produced a revolutionary intellectual community that had been operating underground in Russia and in the Western cities of France, Germany, and Sweden. These men were highly educated in a system of thought developed by Karl Marx and Friedrich Engels in England and Germany during the mid-1800s.

The Legacy of Karl Marx

Socialism. Communism. Capitalism. Marxism. Leninism. Stalinism.

All of these concepts are based on complex systems of thought and are open to many different interpretations. It goes beyond the scope of this book to define these terms properly. Since they are used here, however, a quick rundown of their definitions must suffice.

In Soviet terminology, socialism and communism, as practiced by a nation, require a few basic prerequisites:

1. ownership of the means of production—factories, businesses, etc.—by the state
2. a redistribution of wealth—the high concentration of money and property is taken from the elite minority and equally distributed to everyone in the country
3. centralization of all national activities including banking, medical care, education, communication, agriculture, and industry into the hands of the state

Capitalism on the other hand, involves private owner-ship of the means of production and distribution of goods and services. It has a multiparty system and a decentral-ized government—power exists on various levels. In the United States, for example, laws and governmental deci-sions are made in the Congress, in state and local offices, as well as in the White House.

According to Marx, who wrote in Germany and En-gland during the Industrial Revolution, private ownership of the means of production creates classes of people—rich, poor, and middle class. Workers, the lower classes, were being taken advantage of by the owners. The owners set wages and working hours and, if the worker wanted to feed his family, the worker had to agree to the owners' terms. The workers would resent this and one day would organize, first into unions, then into groups of unions, and finally into a workers' party. With the power gained in numbers, the workers could demand better living condi-tions and higher wages. Finally, tensions would mount as the ruling elite began to fight against the demands made on them by the workers for more and more equality. A violent struggle would take place, and the workers, outnumbering the owners, would win. Socialism would be attained. When the redistribution of wealth and owner-ship takes place, the government is centralized, and education, medical care, and housing would be made available to everyone from the state. A "classless" soci-ety would result. When classlessness has been achieved in both the system and in the minds and attitudes of the people, the state is no longer needed. Commu-nism would now exist. According to a strict read-ing of Marxist doctrine, no country has yet achieved com-munism.

Marx felt that this succession of events was inevitable. It would take place because capitalism was a system doomed to fail. One by one, nations would succumb to socialism—not by force from other countries, but from within, through the struggles of its own working class people. The countries that had already attained socialism should do everything they could to promote the workers' awareness of their plight, and help them win the struggle. But the struggle would take place whether help from the outside was offered or not.

It must be said that Karl Marx devised these theories in an honest attempt to find a solution to the problems faced by society in the 1800s. In his time, during the Industrial Revolution, people were first faced with factories and industry. Working conditions were unsafe. There were no child labor laws. Health insurance, unemployment compensation—none of these measures had yet been enacted. The worker was indeed mercilessly used by most owners of industry.

However, many men would use Marx's theories and name to devise their own systems of government and put themselves in power. Many people feel that Marxist philosophy has been betrayed by the system in the Soviet Union. There are as many interpretations of Marxism, perhaps, as there are revolutionaries. One such revolutionary was Vladimir Lenin.

The Revolution and Its Aftermath

The October Revolution, which installed Lenin as the head of the new Soviet government, also provoked a brutal civil war, which embroiled the already exhausted country in a four-year battle. This further depleted its natural resources, slowing its economy and exacting a high cost in human life. Many atrocities were committed, including the establishment of a secret police force responsible for much brutality and death. It was at the end of this bitter time that Andrei Sakharov was born, on May 21, 1921, in Moscow.

Moscow remained relatively untouched by the strife that surrounded it. Sakharov's immediate family, too, made the transition from Russian to Soviet life fairly well. According to Maksudov, a Soviet *demographer* (one who studies population statistics), "Seven members of the [Sakharov] family took part in World War I, while later five persons—four men and a woman—participated in the Civil War . . . Four members of the family died of typhus and famine during the Civil War."

Sakharov's father was a well-known and respected physicist and author of a number of popular physics textbooks. He was also a rather talented classical pianist, earning a living playing the piano in a silent movie theater during the Civil War. Sakharov fondly remembers hearing him play the music of Chopin, Grieg, Beethoven, and Scriabin at home.

Sakharov's paternal grandmother was the focal point of the household, and he remembers her for her strength and wisdom. He has written that his youth was a remarkably happy and secure one, due to the closeness of his family, many of whom shared a communal apartment in Moscow with him. "From childhood, I lived in an atmosphere of decency, mutual help, a liking for work and respect for the mastery of one's chosen profession."

Throughout his childhood, Andrei had been intrigued by math and physics, at which he was especially gifted. This was due in part, no doubt, to the fact that he was educated at home by his physicist father.

At the time Andrei graduated from high school with honors in 1938, the world, and in particular his own country, had changed dramatically. The father of the revolution, Vladimir Lenin, died in 1924, and within three years, Joseph Stalin had eliminated all opposition and became supreme ruler of the Soviet Union. A shrewd and cruel man, he would rule Russia with an iron fist for three decades, changing the face of world politics forever.

CHAPTER TWO

The Institution of Terror

W hat might have happened to Russia and, in fact, to the fate of international relations, if Joseph Stalin had not become the leader of the Soviet Union can only be imagined. If a kinder man, less obsessed with power, had taken up the reins of government when Vladimar Lenin died, the unique experiment of the Russian Revolution may have taken a drastically different course. Unfortunately, it is a fact of life that from 1927 until his death in 1953, Stalin was the dominating force in the Soviet Union.

Stalin and the Revolution

He was born Joseph Vissarionovich Djugashvili in 1879 to peasant parents in the Georgian section of Russia. During much of his childhood, Stalin seemed an unlikely candidate for the leader of a major power. He was a bright, obedient student, later going to study for the priesthood at a theological seminary. His years at the seminary, located in a major city, brought him into contact with revolutionary ideas from the West in the form of books, periodicals, and conversations with local intellectuals. He was expelled from school in 1899, after a number of warnings about his disrespectful behavior, reading of "unsanctioned books," and, according to Stalin himself, spreading the ideas of Marxism. From that time on, he was a committed communist.

Unlike Lenin and others of the revolutionary movement in Russia, Stalin had never traveled outside his country, nor was he noted for his intellectual capabilities. He was instead practical and shrewd, a hard worker extremely dedicated to the cause of radical change. He even spent a number of years in a Siberian prison for his activities against the Tsarist regime. It was through his hard work that he drew the attention of the top men in the revolutionary organization, becoming the protégé of Vladimir Lenin. Through his ruthless ambition, he secured himself a position in the ruling body of the new government after the Civil War. And it was through both violence and political manuevering that he eliminated all opposition to his rule. After Lenin's death in 1924, he became General Secretary, perhaps the most powerful office in the Soviet Union.

As we have seen in the previous chapter, the country Stalin inherited from Lenin was fraught with enormous problems. He immediately set two main goals: to overcome Russia's desperate economic problems and to secure his rule over the country.

Facing severe famine in the years 1927–28, Stalin's first priority was to stimulate his country's agricultural sector. Since a financial boycott of Russia had started after the revolution, food could not be imported. Besides, no capital funds were available to pay for this importation should the opportunity exist.

It was then that Stalin first devised and put into effect a plan of *collectivization* of agriculture. Small private farms, which numbered over twenty-five million, were taken from their owners and run by the state. Smaller farms were combined and made into huge communal farms. This method was supposed to increase the farms' capacities. While collectivization is an integral part of any communist system, Stalin forced it on his people with characteristic harshness. In the words of historian Isaac Deutscher in his biography of Stalin, the process had

> degenerated into a military operation, a cruel civil war. Rebellious villagers were surrounded by machine guns and forced to surrender. Masses of *kulaks* [middle-class farmers] were deported to remote, unpopulated lands in Siberia. Their homes, barns and farm implements were turned over to the collective farms—Stalin himself put the value of their property at over 400 million rubles.

In industry, too, Stalin pushed for vast increases in output. In fact, the farms that had been so painfully reorganized desperately needed equipment in order to run. Tractors, other heavy machinery, and farm implements had to be manufactured. In addition, Russia needed to rearm to make up for what was lost during World War I. Factories all over the country were set into frantic motion. New ones were built. All of this new industry pointed out the lack of available natural resources—coal, oil, electricity, skilled labor—that the Soviet Union had in rich, largely untapped, supply. Enormous efforts were made to develop them quickly. The country was plunged into a fever of activity. The physical burden was placed upon the backs of the very same people who had risen out of their poverty under the Tsars to fight in the revolution.

Hungry, exhausted after over a decade of war, the

Lenin, the founder of the Soviet Union . . .

. . . and Stalin, the leader who ruled his country with an iron fist for nearly thirty years. *(Courtesy AP/Wide World Photos)*

people of Russia could hardly stand the burden placed upon them by their relentless leader. Many rebelled against the very government they had helped install.

The Beginning of Repression

In order for the new leadership to protect its position, it felt it had to repress its people—to control them so strictly that they could no longer express their dissatisfaction. Stalin introduced harsh repressive measures: the secret police and the *gulags* (forced labor camps where hundreds of thousands of men and women were sent to suffer, many to die), mass executions, and total censorship. So began Stalin's Reign of Terror that would last until World War II and mark the face of Russian life forever after. The cost in human lives was staggering. According to demographer Maksudov, the Terror took the lives of almost half the men born before the revolution and was the cause of death of two-thirds of the men who died between 1920 and 1943.

The secret police (which under the Tsars had been called the *Okhrana,* under Lenin the *Cheka,* under Stalin the GPU, the NKVD, and now the KGB) spied for the government on its own people. Agents were, and still are, in every neighborhood, school, and workplace. In addition to effectively revealing those who don't agree with the government, they also provide another function. One of Stalin's most damaging legacies is the fear invoked in his own people—a deep suspicion of both each other and of the world around them.

This fear of things foreign has its roots deep in Russian history—not only in the necessary protection of its open borders, but also in other ways. The Tsars had been fearful of revolutionary ideas coming from Western Europe. The fact that the Western democracies funded counter-revolutionary forces during the revolution gave the new Soviet leadership cause to fear the West, too. Stalin would make his people fear it even more. In order to protect his own power while demanding more and more from his already exhausted population, he "presented to the Russian people their miserable standard of living as the height of socialist achievement," as Isaac Deutscher expressed it. This meant, of course, that Russians could not be allowed to compare their own situation with that of their Western counterparts who, for the most part, were enjoying a much higher standard of living.

It was then that a policy forbidding the average citizen to travel outside the country or to read about foreign life in books and magazines was imposed. The restriction of information extended to books about Russia's own ancient and more recent past, including novels like Boris Pasternak's *Doctor Zhivago,* published in 1958 and still banned in the Soviet Union today.

Throughout the 1930s, the Terror intensified, claiming thousands upon thousands of lives and instilling a fear and suspicion in the Russian people and their leaders that helps explain their behavior today. Stalin's plan to industrialize his country, it must be said, succeeded to a large degree. With a paranoid eye to catching up to the West, Stalin both pushed his people forward and held them down, with an equally iron fist.

World War II and Further Devastation

Then, in 1939, a rearmed Germany, ruled by the tyrant dictator Adolf Hitler, forced the world into a war that changed the map and set the stage for modern international relations. Two countries, uneasy allies during the war, would emerge as mortal enemies. Both had largely isolated themselves between the two world wars, concentrating on their internal affairs. The United States was, at the beginning of the war, a largely untried power. At the end, she emerged the victorious, fully industrialized leader of the free world. Her economy had boomed during and after the war. Her losses, in lives and capital, were minimal compared with the other nations that fought. Her allies, including the Soviet Union, had sustained heavy losses, economically and in human life.

The other country that emerged was the Soviet Union. It had conquered, and was to keep under its control, Eastern bloc of European nations—Poland, Czechoslovakia, Yugoslavia, Bulgaria, Hungary, and East Germany. But the price the Soviet Union paid for victory was, once again, enormous. According to recent Western estimates, over twenty million Russians were killed in the war, hundreds of thousands more wounded, and all areas of industry devastated.

Once again, too, Stalin would exact payment for these losses from his already weary people. They would pay with their lives and their spirits. They would get very little in return. A huge, impenetrable bureaucracy, with a privileged set of rulers, was entrenching itself. They would continue this repression and isolation from ideas and outside influence long after this cruel dictator had left the scene.

Beginning of the Cold War

But meanwhile, the face of international relations had changed. Stalin, anxious to appear strong before what he perceived to be a hostile world, could not admit to the devastation his country had sustained. He would then appear weak. Therefore, to avoid revealing damaging statistics, he refused to take part in the Marshall Plan, which was devised by the United States to help those countries ravaged by the war. The Eastern bloc countries that had come under Soviet domination also needed aid, but Stalin especially did not want the West interfering there. The more contact his people had with the West, the more chance they would have to compare their life-styles. With that comparison could very well come dissatisfaction and rebellion. The repression and isolation continued.

The Arms Race Begins

One other major piece of the international puzzle, one that represents the greatest threat to human beings in history, was also introduced at this critical time. On August 6, 1945, the United States exploded an atomic bomb on the Japanese city of Hiroshima. Two days later, another bomb was dropped on Nagasaki. The devastation, the loss of life, the sheer power of the weapon was unlike anything the world had ever seen. It brought the war between the United States and Japan to a close almost immediately. The world was aghast.

When the war began, Andrei Sakharov had just turned twenty and was studying at Moscow University. His classes were evacuated when the fighting threatened Moscow, and he spent two years in the remote desert city of Ashkhabad in the Soviet republic of Turkmenia. Sakharov completed his studies, with honors, in 1942. He has written that he, like so many of his fellow countrymen, had wished to join in the fight against the Germans. But that was not to be. He, along with other promising young scientists, was sent to a munitions factory that manufactured artillery shells and other weapons for the Soviet army. Here he would distinguish himself by inventing new and more efficient methods of quality control. He received the first of many citations from the government for his work.

After the war was over, he returned to Moscow to continue his scientific studies and studied under world-renowned theoretical physicist Igor Evenevich Tamm at the Lebedev Physics Institute. In 1947, he received a degree, comparable to our Ph.D., for his work on cosmic-ray theory.

At this time, Sakharov married his first wife, Klavidia. The couple would have three children in the years that followed, but this family would live a far from normal life. For after the United States dropped its atomic bombs over Japan, Stalin would not rest until the Soviet Union had exploded a similar weapon and then exceeded the United States in nuclear technology. Appointing the shrewd Lavrenti Beria, the chief of secret police, to head the new nuclear arms program, Stalin recruited the best physicists in the country. Andrei Sakharov, at the age of twenty-six, was one of them.

CHAPTER THREE

Sakharov and the Bomb

S talin had to work quickly. The Soviet Union was at least five years behind the United States. In 1940 Soviet physicists, working under Igor Kurchatov, had proven that the chain reaction for an atomic explosion could be achieved. The war, however, intervened. Necessary manpower and materials had been diverted to the war effort. After Hiroshima and Nagasaki, though, Stalin would spare no expense. Massive funds, desperately needed in other sectors of a depleted economy, were diverted to the new weapons program. The complicated and intricate scientific conditions under which an atomic reaction (fission) can take place were finally met—the first Soviet atomic bomb was successfully exploded on December 25, 1946. The arms race had begun.

The Soviet Hydrogen Bomb

But Stalin had a plan to surpass the Americans in military technology by developing an altogether different, and much more powerful, weapon—the hydrogen bomb. The best and brightest young scientists were organized by

Beria for this highly sensitive project. Few refused. Those who did, like courageous Pyotr Kapitsa, were fired from their positions and were unable to work for a number of years. Scientists in the program worked under close scrutiny and intense pressure. Sakharov himself felt honored to take part, later recalling,

> I felt subjectively that I was working for peace, that my work would help foster a balance of power and that it would be useful to the Soviet people and even, to some extent, mankind as a whole. . . . Carried away by the immensity of the task, I worked very strenuously, and became the author or coauthor of several key ideas.

The processes undertaken to develop these ideas and the internal structure of the secret laboratories are still largely unknown to the Western world. Dr. Sakharov himself refuses to speak about any of his classified military work, vowing never to betray state secrets. We do know, however, that the first Soviet hydrogen bomb exploded on August 12, 1953, two months after Stalin died.

A Life of Isolation

The twenty years Sakharov would spend working in the weapons program were years in which he came and went through his personal life like a shadow. His family was moved to an apartment provided by the government in Moscow, but he himself was rarely there. He worked in a secret laboratory in Moscow only for a short time. Then he moved to the distant regions of Central Asia and the Urals to work in other secret installations. He was guarded twenty-four hours a day by KGB agents, as a protective measure, even while vacationing. He was not allowed to speak of his work to anyone who did not share his top-security clearance, including his wife. He could not leave the country under any circumstances, nor speak or write to any foreigners. He lived a life of profound isolation, away from any distractions and under constant tension.

But he was also highly rewarded for his service, loyalty, and performance. He received extremely high wages, as well as privileges, including special food, clothing, and other material goods reserved for the elite. He was given a *dacha,* country house, as well as the apartment in Moscow—a grand luxury in a country where the average citizen lives in a communal apartment with at least one other family.

Sakharov also was awarded the most prestigious prizes and commendations available in the Soviet Union, including both the Stalin and Lenin Prizes and, the highest of all, the Hero of Socialist Labor, three times. He was also the youngest member ever to be elected to the esteemed Academy of Sciences. Only thirty-two years old when elected, it was indeed an honor. The membership also carried with it its own set of privileges and salaries.

Sakharov was, in fact, at the pinnacle of Soviet society. He had helped bring the Soviet Union into the nuclear age and successfully compete militarily with the West. It is likely that had he continued to concentrate solely on his scientific studies, he would have lived in this comfort for the rest of his life.

Sakharov's career, however, would take a drastically different turn. For not only was he a brilliant scientist, he was, and remains, a man of conscience. He feels that he must speak his thoughts, no matter what the consequences.

In the years that followed the first U.S. atomic explosion in 1945 and the Soviet hydrogen bomb explosion in 1953, nuclear devices continued to be developed and tested. It was during this time that Sakharov began to question the use of nuclear weapons and the effect they had on the human race and the environment. His privileged position in the scientific and military world gave him a unique overview of the problems involved. As he later recalled,

> As a theoretical scientist and inventor, relatively young and not a party member, I was not involved in administrative responsibilities and was exempt from party discipline. My position enabled me to know and see a great deal. It compelled me to feel my own responsibility and, at the same time, I could look upon this whole perverted system as something of an outsider. All this prompted me . . . to reflect in general terms on the problems of peace and mankind, and in particular on the problems of thermonuclear war and its aftermath.

The Birth of a Dissident

In 1955, Sakharov first spoke out to a Soviet official, Marshal Nedelin, expressing his hope that the weapons now being tested would never be used. Sakharov received the sort of defensive reply he would encounter again and again from the Soviet bureaucracy. Nedelin responded to Sakharov's honest fears by remarking that their leaders could get along very well without advice from the likes of him.

Fear and doubt, however, continued to plague the now thirty-four-year-old scientist. He felt more and more his own individual responsibility for these new devices. He worried constantly about the dangers of continued nucle-

37

ar testing, knowing the damage that could result. "As is well known," he later wrote, "the absorption of the radioactive products of nuclear explosions by the billions of people inhabiting the Earth leads to an increase in the incidence of several diseases and birth defects. . . . Because of the fallout of the radioactive products of a nuclear explosion in the atmosphere, every megaton exploded claims thousands of unknown victims. . . ." Privately, he attempted to persuade Khrushchev, who became the Soviet leader after Stalin's death, to stop the tests in 1958. He did this by persuading the man who now headed the program, Igor Kurchatov, to relay his warning about the dangers of continued testing. The message was ignored and the tests continued.

Also in 1958, Sakharov took his first public stand on a major question of public policy. The American journalist and expert on Soviet affairs, Harrison E. Salisbury, in his foreword to *Sakharov Speaks,* a collection of the scientist's philosophical works, recounts this incident in detail. Sakharov and a colleague, Zeldovich, wrote an open letter to General Secretary Khrushchev opposing a series of educational reforms then being considered. The plan was to interrupt a student's education when he or she was fifteen or sixteen years old. The student would then perform two or three years of practical work—in a factory, for instance. Sakharov and Zeldovich argued that a mathematics or physics student had his best, most productive years relatively early in life, and therefore should be exempt from this practice. Khrushchev did listen to Sakharov this time, and math/physics students were given special treatment.

So began Sakharov's long journey as an outspoken member of a society that punishes those who voice opinions that run counter to government policy. Once again, in 1962, he spoke out against a series of nuclear tests. Despite his insistence that they were not only harmful but also unnecessary, the tests were conducted. Sakharov later told Hedrick Smith of *The New York Times*, "I could not stop something I knew was wrong and unnecessary. It was terrible. I had an awful sense of powerlessness. After that, I was a different man. It was a basic break."

The Khrushchev Thaw

As things changed with Sakharov in the mid-1950s, so had things changed for the Soviet Union. Joseph Stalin, who had ruled this mighty country for nearly all of its first three decades, died on March 5, 1953. Nikita Sergeyevich Khrushchev, a long-time member of the Soviet government, emerged as the new leader. He would take that country through a series of changes and reforms that would last for eleven years, until he was deposed in 1964. It was an era that would come to be known as the "Khrushchev Thaw."

While the extent of Khrushchev's reforms is still being debated by historians and Soviet analysts, it cannot be denied that he did much to bring a feeling of hope to Russia, in the hearts of his countrymen and in the eyes of the world.

Under his leadership, millions of citizens were released from labor camps, prisons, and exile—perhaps as many as eight million. He exposed Stalin as the monster he had been and the crimes against the Soviet people he had committed. By doing this, he gained some trust in his own government from his people and the world. Khrushchev also worked to change the harsh system of farm collectivization Stalin initiated. Thousands of Jews were allowed to emigrate (change their residence) to Israel. Foreign policy became more open—Khrushchev traveled all over the

Khrushchev, the leader who brought hopes of change into an arena of international tension. *(Courtesy AP/Wide World Photos)*

world to meet with leaders of communist and democratic countries alike, even visiting the United States.

And there was a resurgence of cultural activity during this time. More journals and books were being published and there was a feeling of intellectual openness to new ideas. Alexander Solzhenitsyn, famous dissident and future winner of the Nobel Prize for Literature, wrote his first novel, *One Day in the Life of Ivan Denisovitch,* at this time; it was a landmark of the new era.

At the same time, there were still harsh criticisms of dissent from the government, frequently resulting in loss of jobs and prestige for the offender. And every magazine, book, or broadcast was subject to strict government censorship. Travel for the average citizen was still restricted. The economy did not improve to any large degree, and most people had a very low standard of living. But, while there were still nowhere near the freedoms one sees and expects in a democratic society,

Khrushchev, in his way, did much to alleviate the all-pervading fear felt by the Soviet people, instilled in them by the horrors of Stalinism. Yet despite this period of change, the basic structure of the system Stalin left behind—the heavily centralized government, the secret police, the inefficient economy—was left basically intact. The life of the average Soviet citizen was a very, very limited one, even under Khrushchev. And after his ouster from office in 1964, the harsh repressive activities would increase under Brezhnev and the leaders who followed him. There would be other periods of thaw and other crackdowns, but the average day would remain a bleak one.

CHAPTER FOUR

Soviet Life: Stability Through Repression

W hen you live in the Soviet Union, you feel you are part of a tremendous machine. In medicine, there is a machine—a life-support machine—to keep those who are critically ill alive. I would compare the average Soviet citizen to a person who's hooked up to this life-support machine. This person knows that oxygen comes through one tube, nutrients through another, and does not have to think about anything at all. This is the way the average Soviet citizen feels about the state. The state for him is a life-support machine. Though it is a miserable life this machine supports, it *does* support it. . . . Of course, one tries to find better ways to use it, but one cannot do anything to change it.

Dr. Valentin Turchin, a Russian scientist and human rights activist expelled from the Soviet Union in 1977, described life in the Soviet Union that way in an interview in February 1985.

In the last decade or so, a number of Western journalists have published fascinating accounts of their long stays as correspondents in Russia—Hedrick Smith and David K. Shipler of *The New York Times,* Robert G. Kaiser of

The Washington Post, and Michael Binyon of *The Times* of London, to name a few. They have brought to us striking glimpses of a world most of us will never get a chance to see. To a large degree, the pictures they paint mirror the statement made above by Dr. Turchin. He went on to say, "Imagine that everything in the United States was owned by one big corporation, including all the land, all the industry and the courts of law. That is the Soviet Union."

Everyday Life

By all accounts, it is a badly organized, inefficient, and corrupt "corporation." The economy is in shambles, the average citizen does not have enough to eat, or access to enough decent housing. There exists an elite class of privileged people—high-ranking members of the Soviet government and Communist Party, certain athletes, artists, and scientists, the KGB—to whom better food, housing, and consumer goods are offered. As we've seen with Dr. Sakharov, these privileges add up to a life quite different from that of even their wealthy American counterparts. Because they are given in secret, they can all be taken away, as quickly as they were given, by the state.

But there is a day-to-day routine, with its common ups and downs, that the Soviet people perform. In many ways, it closely resembles our own. Russians shop, listen to music, save up to buy a car, send their children off to school, go to work. They fall in love and nurture their hopes and dreams.

The basic standard of living, however, despite largely successful efforts in past years to improve it, is still considerably below our own. For example, a large part of every day is spent waiting in lines—for food, for the scarce entertainment, for consumer goods. In his excellent book, *Russia,* Robert Kaiser, recounts a typical shopping experience:

> To buy bread means waiting in line at the bread store, paying in advance the exact price of the loaves you want, taking the receipt for that amount to a second line at the bread counter, then finally trading your receipt with a saleswoman for bread. The same procedure is repeated in every kind of shop—for sour cream and yogurt, for cheese and salami, for cabbage and canned peas.

Stores are notoriously understocked. One may wait in line all day, only to find that the item needed had been sold out hours before. The average person eats fresh meat only once a week in major cities; in the countryside, even less often. The wait to buy a car is from one to five years.

Despite enormous spurts in building in the past thirty years, the housing situation is still deplorable. More than 25 percent of the population still live in communal apartments. Those who are privileged enough to live privately reside in tiny one-room apartments, and feel lucky for that. The housing shortage is so severe in Moscow that, according to Robert Kaiser, "it is not uncommon for divorced couples to continue living together because neither can find new accomodations."

Women make up 51 percent of the labor force, and 92 percent of all working-age women either work or study. Since the ravages of World War II claimed so many men, women make up 54 percent of the population. Moreover, women constitute about 70 percent of all doctors (who are notoriously underpaid) and virtually no factory could operate without female labor. While there is a certain amount of equality in the workplace, mostly due to economic necessity, equality at home remains lacking. Russian women too are expected not only to have full-time jobs but to keep house as well!

Education and Medical Care

Education and medical care fare a bit better than consumer goods, housing, and women's rights, though to what extent is a hotly debated subject.

School begins when a child is seven years old, a year or two later than in most Western countries. But this time is made up by the intensity of the training. School runs six days a week, from September 1 to May 30, with only a few short holidays. A student is required to attend school until the age of seventeen. Pupils are taught according to strict party discipline. Emphasis is on memorization and mathematics—very little attention is paid to creative or independent thinking. As Robert Kaiser observes,

Like so many aspects of Soviet life, education is highly formalized and narrowly practical. Its goal is *not* to produce men and women of great intellectual breadth, originality or creativity. On the contrary, none of this is sought. Soviet education is supposed to supply the country with specialists who can make [the economy] work. . . .

But in a country in which the majority of people were illiterate as recently as fifty years ago, it cannot be denied that enormous gains have been made.

Free medical care is another one of a group of economic rights guaranteed under the Soviet constitution. This free treatment, by most accounts, is erratic and unpredictable. Like almost everything else in the Soviet Union, hospitals are understaffed and undersupplied. Doctors are overworked and underpaid. Their job lacks the prestige it has here in the United States; hence, the profession does not always attract the brightest candidates. Because of a lack of communication and scientific exchange between the Soviet Union and the more advanced West, medical technology lags behind the West by a number of years.

The Communist Party

While communist ideology and propaganda pervades every sector of everyday life in the Soviet Union, the Communist Party itself is a relatively small organization. It has approximately fifteen million official members, about 7 percent of the population. Robert Kaiser reports that in certain groups this percentage is much higher: More than half of the men over thirty with a college education are party members, and so are more than 99 percent of all members of government. To get to the top in the Soviet Union, it is almost imperative that one become a member. Exceptions to this rule frequently include prominent artists and scientists (Sakharov himself was never a member). You must be invited to join by another party member, mainly on the recommendation of the Komsomol leadership—those who run the Youth Communist League.

The Youth Communist League is an institution of the Soviet government whose purpose is to educate its young members (fourteen to seventeen years old) with party philosophy. It is obligatory for everyone to participate, even if he or she does not intend to join the Communist Party. Otherwise, one could very well be barred from higher education, jobs, even apartments later on in life. It is here young Soviets are taught the vigorous party rules, regulations, and philosophy that will take them through their lives. It is here as well, in day-to-day schooling, that the average citizen learns the "world according to the party."

The KGB

By Western estimates, the Soviet secret police has 90,000 officers in Russia and abroad. These are men and women whose responsibility is "state security." All ordinary crimes, those that have no possible relation to state security, such as theft, homicide, assault, etc., are taken care of by the militia of the Ministry of Internal Affairs, a force several times larger. Like the party, the KGB is virtually everywhere. Each college, factory, and enterprise in the country has its First Department, a secretive office in charge of personnel and security, manned by representatives of the KGB. Every town and city has its own branch.

But the real power of the agency depends on its unofficial staff, an army of paid and unpaid informers. These informers are everywhere, listening, watching, and reporting everything they hear and see. Some have been recruited for money, others to avoid imprisonment for committing a crime, some because it is simply in their nature. The effect of this widespread spying is a fear and suspicion of Russians—by other Russians.

During Stalin's Terror, the hero of the country was Pavel Morozov, a fifteen-year-old peasant boy. According to the famous story, Pavel's father was planning to resist the forced collectivization imposed upon his village by Stalin. Pavel informed the authorities about what his father intended to do. His father was then taken for "questioning" and shot to death. The father's friends, the boy's neighbors, killed Pavel. Pavel was made into a hero.

He had died for the revolutionary cause by reporting on his father, causing his execution.

Although conditions have vastly improved since the Stalin era, the possibility of betrayal—by even those closest to you—pervades the atmosphere.

Stability Reigns

Despite its drawbacks, however, the Soviet system is a stable one. As one worker told Hedrick Smith, "I never have to worry . . . I can walk out of my institute and get another job . . . I will make the same money, 220 rubles . . . I can count on my 220 rubles. That is the big difference. I don't have to worry about the future, you do." And Roy Medvedev, Soviet dissident and human rights activist, told Italian correspondent Piero Ostellino in 1977,

> While we're behind the Western nations in civil rights, we have no unemployment or galloping inflation; the state holds the cost of prime necessities down to an extremely low level: housing, public transportation, bread, milk, potatoes and so on. We have free medical care and free education, obligatory to the age of seventeen. The right to social security is guaranteed to the sick and elderly. We cannot deny these benefits exist. . . .

Perhaps this is why, by all accounts, the average Soviet citizen is relatively satisfied with his or her life. Compared to life forty years ago, conditions have improved enormously. The older citizens remember the violence and hardships of the 1930s and 1940s. Those younger, who have nothing to compare their life to, find they have, in basic terms, enough to eat and a general sense of security.

Dissent

But there is another section of society whose members are not satisfied with their lot in life. These individuals want more than the bare necessities of practical life: they desire freedom of speech, the freedom to travel and live wherever they want, the freedom to read and write whatever material suits their tastes. Those who speak out about these desires and demand their rights to them are known as *dissidents,* those who "think differently."

There have been dissidents in the Soviet Union since the revolution. The revolutionaries themselves had been dissidents under the Tsars. Sometimes numbering in the thousands, sometimes just a few dozen, Soviet dissidents represent a challenge to the politics of repression practiced by their government. Many have been silenced, but the movement continues. Andrei Sakharov has one of the clearest voices of protest. He began his song of justice in the changing world of the nuclear age.

"The most important conditions for international trust and security are the openness of society, the observation of the civil and political rights of man. . . " Andrei Sakharov *(Courtesy Efrem Yankelvich)*

CHAPTER FIVE

Sakharov and Dissent

The Moscow Test Ban Treaty, signed by President Kennedy of the United States and General Secretary Khrushchev of the Soviet Union, was put into effect in 1963 and remains a basic part of our arms agreements today. Andrei Sakharov, concerned about the danger of continued radiation fallout, had written to the Soviet leadership proposing just such a ban on the testing of nuclear weapons and, he would later write with characteristic modesty, "It could be that my initiative was of some help in that historic act." Indeed there is every reason to believe that his stature in Soviet and international science finally influenced his leaders.

Sakharov's Fight Against Lysenko

Later that year, Sakharov became increasingly concerned about a fellow scientist, biologist Trofin Lysenko. Since the mid-1930s, Lysenko's theory of genetics had ruled an entire branch of science in the Soviet Union. He believed that circumstances in the environment could provoke changes in a living organism, and that these changes could be inherited by the next generation of that organism. He had worked in agriculture and, using different varieties of wheat, tried to prove that he could change a fast-maturing spring wheat strain into a high-protein winter wheat simply by exposing spring seeds to frigid winter conditions. He insisted that genes, which we know to be the key to heredity, did not, in fact, have much to do with heredity at all.

By all accounts, it was a ridiculous theory. Lysenko, however, had managed to convince not only Stalin, but Khrushchev as well. His brand of genetics reigned over both agriculture and the biological sciences for over twenty years. Because, as Valentin Turchin has described, the Soviet Union is like a huge company owned by the government, science too was subject to the whims of its leaders. Stalin, believing in Lysenko's brand of "Marxist" biology, removed all members of the scientific community who openly disputed Lysenkoist biology. Nikolai Vavilov, the brilliant geneticist who promoted the accepted and proven Mendelian theory of hereditary, died in a prison camp in 1942. Soviet biology and agriculture were set back years because of Lysenko, a ludicrous, but powerful, man.

Physics and genetics were becoming more closely related as research into the effects of nuclear radiation continued. The research inevitably showed that the direct effects of radiation on the genes resulted in birth defects in the next generation of the organisms exposed. Sakharov's own studies, including a groundbreaking paper, "The Radioactive Carbon of Nuclear Explosions and Nonthreshold Biological Effects," published in 1953, proved to Sakharov the damage that was being done by Lysenkoism.

In 1964, two of Lysenko's followers were attempting to become members of the esteemed Academy of Sciences.

Sakharov and a number of his fellow physicists were adamantly opposed to it, and made their positions known to the authorities, including Khrushchev himself. Khrushchev, on the other hand, was determined that Lysenko's followers, N.I. Nuzhdin and G.V. Nikolsky, be admitted to the Academy. If they were not, Khrushchev would see the Academy dissolved and the dissenters punished.

Despite the enormous threat, Sakharov and his mentor and colleague Igor Tamm led the fight. Luckily for Sakharov and, indeed, the Academy, Khrushchev was ousted from office before action against them could be taken. Valery Soifer, a biologist and human rights activist still living in the Soviet Union, later wrote, "That struggle brought to light something in him [Sakharov] that singled him out from among many colleagues: a capacity for public activity, a lack of fear in the face of pressure of any kind, and adherence to principles above everything. . . . This was perhaps his first test of strength." It was also the first time that Sakharov's name appeared in the Soviet press linked with an "anti-government cause;" he was denounced as "incompetent and naive" by Mikhail Ol'Shansky, the president of the All-Union Academy of Agricultural Sciences.

For this kind of activity, Sakharov would pay a price, the total of which would not be exacted for a number of years. For now, he was dropped a few notches from his top-security status, thereby losing nearly half his salary. This action, however, provided him with a sort of release —he could associate more freely with his colleagues. His scientific work, which was extending from the tiny world of the atom to broader questions about the origin and nature of the universe, could now be published in public journals.

53

Brezhnev and the Threat of Re-Stalinization

The ouster of Khrushchev, which was probably prompted by his failures in economic policy, marked the beginning of yet another painful period in Soviet history. While Khrushchev's reign certainly had its drawbacks, as evidenced so well by the trauma in science caused by Lysenko, it also was a time of cultural and intellectual stimulation—if not in fact, then at least in spirit.

Leonid Brezhnev, who would rule Russia for eighteen years, was, perhaps even more than Stalin, responsible for transforming his country into a true superpower. Russia would now have military and political interests that would have only one rival: the United States. Brezhnev's reign would span the administrations of five American presidents: Lyndon Johnson, Richard Nixon, Gerald Ford, Jimmy Carter, and, for two years, Ronald Reagan.

Brezhnev would hold the reins on the internal affairs of his country quite tightly. Any relaxation of the strictures on freedom of speech and exchange of ideas felt under Khrushchev was immediately tightened. During the opening months of the Brezhnev administration, rumors circulated around Moscow that Stalin would once again be made a hero, despite the fact that under Khrushchev, the terrifying extent of his crimes had been made clear. This signaled a warning to those who were listening, and objections were immediately raised in the intellectual and academic communities.

Andrei Sakharov and two other colleagues, Pyotr Kapitsa and Igor Tamm, joined other liberal-minded artists, writers, and scientists in appealing to their government to put an end to re-Stalinization. Stalin was not "rehabilitated"(once again made into a national hero), though what effect this protest had is not known.

In the same year, a new law came into effect, Article 190-1 of the Criminal Code, which set a three-year labor camp sentence for the "circulation of fabrications known to be false which defame the Soviet state and social system." This was a law that would be used over and over again to persecute those who were even slightly critical of the Soviet government.

Shortly before, in 1965, two young writers, Andrei Sinyavsky and Yuli Daniel, had been arrested. They had been charged with illegally publishing "anti-Soviet" works abroad, under pseudonyms. When their works, which were relatively mild satire, had not been allowed to be printed in the Soviet Union, where everything published must be approved by government censors, they sent their works out of the country. For this, Sinyavsky was sentenced to seven years in a labor camp. Daniel received a five-year sentence.

A huge protest against this action was mounted, and Sakharov joined in. He was beginning to understand more and more what the lack of freedom could mean for his country. He later wrote, "For the first time, my own fate became intertwined with the fate of that group of people—a group that was small but very weighty on the moral (and I would say historical) plane—who subsequently became known as dissenters."

The punishment for publically disagreeing with the Soviet government, as was seen by the sentences exacted upon Sinyavsky and Daniel (only two of thousands upon thousands), had not disappeared after Stalin's Terror. Nor did Khrushchev's "thaw," such as it was, do anything to change that. The punishment can be forced labor, prison, harassment of family and friends, internal exile to Siberia or other closed parts of the country, even expulsion from the Soviet Union altogether.

When asked why some have the courage to risk such

severe penalties while most remain silent, Dr. Valentin Turchin put it this way:

> In mathematical terms, we distinguish between necessary and "sufficient" conditions that are needed to prove a theory. The sufficient conditions—what will finally make someone give up everything to speak out—I can't define.
>
> But I can give you a "necessary" condition: You don't become a dissident unless you have a certain "metaphysical quality of mind." You must believe in some transcendent values, in something more than day-to-day existence. Otherwise, from a practical standpoint, to become a dissident makes no sense.

Andrei Sakharov does believe in values that go beyond the practical life he had lived so comfortably as a national hero. He would tell Hedrick Smith of *The New York Times* in a 1974 interview, "The atomic question was always half-science, half-politics. The atomic issue was a natural path into political issues. What matters is that I left conformism. It is not important on what question. After that first break, everything later was natural."

Indeed, he could not conform to a life surrounded by injustice. And he felt he had to speak out against these injustices and express his humanistic values. He began to formulate specific solutions and theories, not only about conditions in the Soviet Union, but about peace, dictatorship, environmental pollution, and the responsibility of scientists to their fellow man.

The publication of his 1968 essay, "Thoughts on Progress, Co-Existence, and Intellectual Freedom," marked a turning point in Sakharov's life, and in the cause of human rights around the world.

CHAPTER SIX

Thoughts on Progress

//T houghts on Progress, Co-Existence, and Intellectual Freedom" was considered throughout the world to be a remarkable document, especially coming from academician Andrei Sakharov—a privileged member of the Soviet elite, father of the hydrogen bomb, a man who had everything to lose by speaking out.

In this article, which was published and distributed *samizdat* (self-published and distributed without the government's knowledge or approval) and smuggled to the West, Sakharov expressed for the first time ideas and basic philosophies he had been developing for years. The fact that many of those years he had been isolated from other thinkers, and from the West altogether, makes the document all the more extraordinary for the intensity of its universal messages.

Sakharov put forth two basic premises. The first is that it is the *division* of mankind—into nations and opposing systems of government—that threatens world peace. The competition and adversity of capitalism and socialism hold back the progress of the world. Every aspect of life is unable to grow, from technology to science to humanitarianism. If the two superpowers could pool their resources, astounding accomplishments for all of mankind could be made.

His second premise is that intellectual freedom is absolutely essential to human society. Without this freedom, all of society runs the risk of being brainwashed by those in power, which could lead to a bloody dictatorship. Intellectual freedom, as Sakharov defined it, must express itself in three ways: "the freedom to obtain and distribute information; freedom for open-minded and unfearing debate; and freedom from pressure by officialdom and prejudices."

The Threat of Nuclear War

Sakharov then divided his essay into two parts—"Dangers" and "The Basis for Hope." Here he further elucidated the plan he had for a world of peace and cooperation.

To Sakharov, the first and most important problem to be solved was the threat of nuclear war. The sheer power of the weapons he himself had helped to create made it impossible to consider using them because, he wrote, "A thermonuclear war cannot be considered a continuation of politics by other means. . . . It would be a means of universal suicide." Therefore, the system of international affairs needed to be changed to avoid one superpower using these dreaded devices against the other. A policy of peaceful co-existence must be attempted, Sakharov thought, whereby each system of government allows the other to live free from any external threat.

Instead of pursuing short-term goals in international politics, he felt that world leaders should put all "concrete aims and local tasks" aside. More important were long-range goals: finding a way to prevent aggravating international tensions and expand the possibilities for peaceful co-existence and cooperation. The wars in Vietnam and the Middle East, he pointed out, were two cases where short-term, selfish goals were obstructing the path of co-existence.

Hunger and Pollution

Two devastating problems facing the modern world— hunger and pollution—cannot be solved, Sakharov remarked, unless each and every developed country cooperates with one another. Hunger, which plagues nearly half the world, could be alleviated if the United States and the Soviet Union put aside their differences and pooled their resources. This would involve a great many sacrifices on the part of every citizen on both sides. In the United States, for instance, Sakharov felt that it would be necessary to "change the psychology of the American citizens so that they will voluntarily and generously support their government and worldwide efforts to change the economy, technology and level of living of millions of people."

Then he suggested that a fifteen-year tax, equal to 20 percent of their national incomes, be imposed on the wealthiest countries in the world. These revenues would be put into a fund for Third World development. Not only would this go a long way toward solving the hunger problem, but it would also cut down on money available for the military. A reduction in the arms race would necessarily follow.

Pollution of the air and water, it was obvious to this informed scientist, could not be solved without an international concentration on the problem. Otherwise, he wrote, "the Soviet Union will poison the United States

with its wastes and vice versa." With peaceful cooperation and pooling of resources, this problem, too, could be
solved. Without it, we would destroy our planet through
selfishness and greed. Long-range goals *had* to be set for
life to continue on earth.

Censorship, Police Dictatorships, Freedom

In this section of the essay, Sakharov spoke mostly to
his own country. He recalled the horrors of Stalinism and
warned against a revival of Stalin's policies and methods.
He warned against making schools simply outlets for
propaganda. He insisted on the essential right of man to
have access to any and all information and ideas, and the
right to speak those ideas without fear. He condemned
most forcefully the Soviet practice of punishing those who
do speak out. Soviet laws, especially those concerning
free speech, were too general, he felt, and open to abuse
by the authorities. He suggested that simple, direct laws
be published, outlining what is and is not acceptable. The
public could then at least understand what they could say,
read, and write without risking punishment.

Without this freedom of thought, Sakharov believed,
Soviet society could never advance at all; certainly not to
the point where it could converge peacefully with the
United States and other democracies. The Soviet people,
through distorted history texts in schools and manipulated
news broadcasts and journals, are brought up fearing and
hating the West and, without access to information about
Americans and their way of life, that fear and hate would
remain and grow.

At that time, in 1968, Sakharov felt strongly that his
vision of the world could come about. He believed that
while, so far, capitalism had given a much higher standard

of living to its people than socialism, true socialism had its own "vitality . . . which has done a great deal for the people materially, culturally and socially and, like no other system, has glorified the moral significance of labor." It was not the system of socialism itself that was holding the Soviet people down, it was the harsh restrictions on their intellectual freedom. He had high hopes that his own country was on its way to liberalizing itself from within, peacefully, so that freedom and democracy could one day flourish.

In fact, in his concluding section, he described a tentative plan for the development of mankind. Admitting that these proposals were in some ways "primitive," he did, however, feel strongly that they should be attempted. Otherwise, the world would never know peace.

The Basis for Hope

The first stage in this ideal development of mankind would involve a vast increase in the practice of democracy in the Soviet Union and other communist countries. Increasingly forceful arguments between two opposing political groups—the Stalinists and the Leninists—would pave the way to a multiparty system like we have in the United States. Because the disagreements between the parties would be open, public, and encouraged, intellectual as well as political freedom would flourish.

The second stage of his plan would take place in the democratic capitalistic countries. Here, the pressure from the good example set by the "new" socialist countries would encourage an increase in social equality and a change in the structure of ownership. This would be a move toward a more complete convergence between the two world powers.

In the third stage, the Soviet Union and the United States, freed from the animosity, competition, and suspicion that had plagued their relationship, would now be able to attack the real problems confronting mankind—hunger, pollution, and the development of the poorer countries in the world.

The fourth stage would lead to the creation of a world government. This government and its people would concentrate on a scientific-technological revolution. Space exploration would flourish, electronics and *cybernetics* (robots) would be expanded, and progress in the biological sciences would lead to new discoveries in all aspects of life.

Sakharov finished this first and most important exploration of his philosophy with a paragraph that challenges the leadership of his own country, making it clear that the first problem to be solved was very close to home:

Every honorable and thinking person who has not been poisoned by narrow-minded indifference will seek to ensure that future development will be along the lines of [peaceful co-existence]. However, only broad, open discussion, without the pressure of fear and prejudice, will help the majority to adopt the correct and best course of action.

Free exchange of ideas is one of the basic principles of democracy, so it is perhaps difficult for us in the United States to see how courageous and insightful this document would seem to those living in the Soviet Union. Sakharov's ideas in this essay are not, it is true, practical ones—ones that can be immediately acted upon—but he did spell out the basic hope and long-range requirements necessary for intellectual freedom throughout the world.

Soviet Reaction

Within weeks after the article was published, Sakharov was barred from all secret work. Harrison Salisbury, in his foreword to *Sakharov Speaks,* described what happened this way:

> Sakharov was discharged from the nuclear weapons program in an action taken with typical Soviet brutality. One morning he arrived at the laboratory as usual in his chauffeur-driven car (one of the privileges of a member of the Academy of Science). But when he approached the working area, the guard refused to admit him, saying that his security clearance had been withdrawn. He was told that he no longer had a job.

One year later, the Soviet government gave him a job, in a relatively minor position for someone of his stature, at the Lebedev Physics Institute. He had returned to the school where his career had begun, where he received his degree in 1947. His whole life changed profoundly.

One of the first things he did was to contribute nearly all his life savings to a government fund for the construction of a cancer hospital and to the Red Cross. This money had come mainly from the high salaries and prizes earned and won from his work connected with weapons research. It is an act about which he would write in 1973, "At that time, I had no personal contacts with people in need of help. Today, I constantly see around me people who need not only protection, but also material help. I often regret my overly hasty gesture."

Indeed, Sakharov would meet many people who would need his help. He would become totally immersed in, and committed to, the cause of freedom and human rights.

Sakharov stands outside a courthouse, during one of the many trials he attended for fellow dissidents. This photo was taken in 1979. *(Courtesy Efrem Yanklevich)*

His generosity and humanitarianism would grow as he learned more and more about the lack of freedom in his country. And he would try to help those who suffered, through his position as a renowned scientist recognized throughout the world.

CHAPTER SEVEN

Two Voices Merge

The next few years, following the publication of "Thoughts," were terribly important ones for Sakharov. His views on the hope for change in the Soviet system and international relations would be transformed. His public life would grow in stature; he would become an international figure.

His personal life would change dramatically as well. It had recently been quite painful. His first wife, Klavidia, died in 1968, after suffering with cancer for a number of years. He was left with three children, two daughters in their early twenties and a young boy of eleven. Although they would live with him until his second marriage in 1971, Sakharov's relationship with his family was, and remains, a difficult one. It had never been close, largely because of the years he spent in isolation, working on top-secret projects. But then, with the death of his wife and his increasing political activities (of which his children did not approve), the break deepened. To this day, they remain estranged, in spirit as well as physical distance.

Sakharov's public life was busier than ever during the early 1970s. It would be a tumultuous decade for him, his country, and the relations between the United States and the Soviet Union.

For Sakharov, it began with an open letter signed by him, Roy Medvedev, an historian and teacher, and physicist Valentin Turchin, to General Secretary Brezhnev. It called for internal reforms to alleviate the heavy censorship and economic stagnation and the introduction of democratic reforms. It supported some basic ideas of socialism, but insisted that if democratic institutions were not introduced, the country's economic, scientific, and cultural growth would cease. The three men never received a reply.

Psychiatry As Punishment

Later in that same year, Sakharov took part in a campaign organized by Roy Medvedev, an outspoken dissident, and other intellectuals and scientists. The campaign was for the release of Zhores Medvedev, Roy's twin brother, from the confines of a state mental hospital. Zhores, a biologist, had spoken out on a continuing basis against censorship and restrictions in travel and emigration. He had also been active, as had Sakharov, in the fight against Lysenkoist biology.

Instead of putting him in jail or exiling him for his "crimes against the state," the authorities took another line of action. Subjecting him to perhaps the most frightening practice of all, they forced him to undergo psychiatric "treatment" in a mental hospital. This use of psychiatric treatment is, unfortunately, an established part of the Soviet system of punishment for political dissidents, "those who think differently."

The prisoner becomes a "patient" and is confined in a hospital for an indefinite amount of time. He is subjected to frequently dangerous treatment—shock therapy, isolation, mind-altering drugs, brainwashing. The practice, which goes against any democratic and humane idea of justice and law, serves the authoritarian regime in a number of ways. First, it portrays the dissident as insane, unable to judge right from wrong. His ideas, therefore, have no meaning—they come from a madman, after all. Second, in a practical way, it keeps the dissident from speaking out, since he is isolated and confined. Third, when and if the dissident is released, he may be unable or unwilling to "think differently" again.

Zhores Medvedev was just one of thousands of those confined, including many others Sakharov has defended. (And Medvedev was one of the lucky ones. The campaign, which focused on his scientific status and was joined by members of the esteemed Academy of Science, was successful. Medvedev was ultimately released. Others are not so lucky.)

The Moscow Human Rights Committee

Sakharov's involvement with the Medvedev case, and others like it, forced him to look more closely at the human rights situation in his own country. His views on the problems confronting mankind evolved because of that involvement. As he told Olle Stenholm, a Swedish correspondent:

My life has been such that I began by confronting global problems and only later more concrete, personal and human ones. . . . When I wrote "Thoughts," I was very far from the basic problems of all the people and of the whole country. I found myself in an extraordinary position of material privilege and isolated from the people. After that, my life began to change in purely personal terms, psychologically. And the process of development simply went further.

Later in 1970, his growing concerns would convince him to form the Moscow Human Rights Committee, along with the physicist Valery Chalidze and Andrei Tverdokhalebov. It was their intention that this group would consider and publicize human rights problems in the Soviet Union, such as forced hospitalization and the issue of discrimination against certain nationalities. The issue of discrimination had become a critical one for the Soviet people. A number of different peoples had come under the power of the Soviet government after the revolution. These different ethnic and national groups had their own cultural and historical identities, quite separate from the Russian one. However, the practice of local traditions was discouraged and people were forced to think of themselves as *Soviets* above anything else. Separate national and ethnic identities would not be tolerated. Each Soviet citizen was issued a passport, with his nationality stamped on it, and travel was restricted, even within the country.

In the case of the Tatars, a people who once lived in the republic of the Crimea, this repression took an even greater toll. In 1944, Stalin had resettled the entire Crimean Tatar population, forcing them to scatter throughout the country, living in isolated communities. To this day, they are not allowed to return. Similar situations exist for other peoples throughout the country.

The repression of these minorities also went against the spirit of democracy that Sakharov felt so deeply. He would speak for them as well, within the Human Rights Committee, and on his own. The committee, in name, still exists in the Soviet Union, but its members have been harassed, fired from their jobs, and worse. In the case of Valery Chalidze, he was forced to leave the country forever. Andrei Sakharov remains in exile in Gorki.

Elena Bonner

Sakharov continued to work hard throughout the summer and fall of 1970. In October he attended the trial of two men, mathematician R. Pimenov and actor B. Vail, who had been accused of distributing material *samizdat* (underground). Groups of protesters, Sakharov among them, stood on the frozen steps of the courthouse, denied entrance to the courtroom. It was here that he met Elena Bonner, a forty-seven-year-old pediatrician and mother of two.

They came from very different backgrounds. They had had very different experiences. But they both had come to the courthouse steps because of an equal commitment to justice. They fell in love almost at first sight. A year later they married.

In many ways, it has been the strength of this extraordinary woman that has kept Sakharov alive and able to work throughout the past fifteen years. Thanks to Kevin Klose, in his book *Russia and the Russians,* and to Tatyana Yankelevich, Elena's daughter now living in the United States, we have a clear picture of her incredible life of courage.

Even the very first hours of her life were remarkable. Her mother, Ruf Bonner, had been working in the Moslem area of the newly formed Soviet Union when she went into labor. A few hours after Elena was born, Ruf was told that a band of Moslem warriors had been seen approaching the hospital. Ruf got up, wrapped her new daughter in a sheet, and took refuge at a friend's home. She later found out that the Moslems had slaughtered everyone who had remained behind.

The Legacy of Repression

Elena's mother, a Jew from eastern Siberia, would also have a life that required huge amounts of courage and spirit. She had come from a community of intellectuals that had been severely discriminated against under the Tsars. Her family had always fought for a just society, and she would instill in her children that same sense of commitment.

Elena's father was Georgi Alikhanov, an Armenian who had settled with his parents in the republic of Georgia after fleeing the Turk invasion of Armenia in 1915. He met Ruf Bonner in Moscow, where they both had come to study at the university. Both of them were lovers of poetry and literature, and Ruf, who now lives with her grandchildren and great-grandchildren in the United States, made sure that her children were instilled with that same love and intellectual curiosity.

Like many other young people, Elena's parents were committed, enthusiastic Communists. Georgi had been the founder of the Armenian Communist Party. Ruf later worked as a party propagandist. They believed in the socialist philosophy and the true idealism they saw around them. After working for the party in the countryside, they moved to Moscow to become members of the Third International. The Comintern, as it was also known, was founded by Lenin to promote world revolution. Hundreds of people from all of Russia and Western Europe came to Moscow to discuss and plan for the spread of communism. Elena later told Kevin Klose that she remembered that time in her early childhood and in her country's early stages of development fondly:

> That generation was completely sincere in its beliefs. There was no speculation, no corruption . . . they all had a completely sincere desire to change things in the world. In our house, Russians and foreigners lived and worked together. We helped them with their Russian language and their social obligations. All believed then . . . absolutely. Everyone was wrapped up in a romantic revolutionaryism. . . . But now it's clear we should have tied ourselves to humanism.

Her family would quickly and harshly learn that revolutionary zeal without safeguards against dictatorship could lead to violence and brutality. Both of Elena's parents were victims of the Stalinist Terror, which claimed the lives not only of those opposed to the revolution, but even those who were its most sincere supporters. Stalin mistrusted everyone around him. Petty intrigues in government became matters of life and death. On May 27, 1937, Elena's father left for work and was never seen again. She has reason to believe he was shot as a traitor, but she has never received official confirmation. Ruf was taken away to a labor camp 15,000 miles east, where she would work and suffer in Stalin's brutal gulags for eight years, then spend nearly nine more in exile.

Elena and her younger brother were sent to Leningrad, where they stayed with an uncle and a grandmother. They lived in constant fear, especially after their uncle was also arrested. Would the children be next? Elena, just sixteen, went to Moscow to plead her case to the authorities. Just in time, Stalin issued a statement in which he said that children should not be held responsible for the crimes of their parents. Elena went back to Leningrad and was studying Russian literature when World War II broke out in 1941. She joined the war effort, working as a nurse in the medical corps.

While serving at the front, Elena suffered severe wounds and a concussion. She spent a few months recovering, and then served four more years. When she was discharged in 1945, she had achieved the rank of lieutenant in the medical corps. But the concussion she had sustained had caused almost complete loss of vision in her right eye and she was losing sight in the left also. For two years, she lived in fear that she would go blind. She spent that time being treated by specialists in Leningrad until her conditioned stablized.

At that time, Elena enrolled at the Leningrad Institute to study medicine, completing the six-year course in 1953. She married her first husband, Ivan Semenov, another doctor, during that time; her first child, daughter Tatyana, was born in 1950, and her son, Alexei, in 1956. The family lived in Leningrad, where Elena worked as a pediatrician.

First Steps Toward Dissidence

While Elena had served her country faithfully during the war and after, she had never joined the Communist Party. She wrote in a biographical piece later published in the United States by Khronika Press, "I never deemed it possible—psychologically—to join the Communist Party while my parents were considered traitors or, to use the phrase current at the time, 'enemies of the people.'" But after Khrushchev released those imprisoned by Stalin and denounced Stalin's crimes against the people, she felt she could believe in her country again. She was made a member of the party in 1965, a decision she would grow to regret as the extent of human rights abuses became clear to her. She would resign her membership in 1972.

Elena's own first steps on the path of dissidence were taken when she was given an opportunity to work as part of a medical team in Iraq. The Middle Eastern country had just undergone a revolution to oust the British monarchy that had ruled there. Khrushchev, ever anxious to influence new governments, sent groups of teachers and medical personnel as an offer of humanitarian aid.

Elena's first taste of foreign life revealed to her both the good and bad points of Soviet life. To see and experience another culture was a liberating experience. Two years later, when she returned to the Soviet Union, she was disappointed at how much the mood of isolation and fear had deepened. When she decided to publish a series of articles about her experiences in Iraq, she was also surprised at how thorough the system of censorship was. But her love for writing, which stemmed from her childhood, grew.

When her marriage to Ivan Semenov ended in 1962 (they were later divorced), she moved to Moscow and found herself in the midst of intense intellectual activity. The Khrushchev Thaw put her in contact with other young writers and intellectuals.

She too felt the shock of Khrushchev's ouster and the harshness of the new regime. Like many of her intellectual compatriots, she would take her views underground. The trial of Sinyavsky and Daniel had signalled the beginning of a new round of repression, and the real revival of an underground dissident movement.

While Sakharov was beginning "Thoughts," Elena was helping to produce a new *samizdat* publication, "Chronicle of Current Events." It would report arrests, trials, and other infringements on freedom of speech and expression. Its first publication coincided with an event in 1968 that

Sakharov and Bonner in Moscow, 1975. *(Courtesy Efrem Yankelevich)*

would further deplete what hope remained for peace and freedom in the Soviet Union—the invasion of Czechoslovakia by Soviet troops. Czechoslovakia, like most of Eastern Europe, was in the Soviet sphere of influence. It had its own government in name, but was expected to take its orders and form its policies through Moscow. When it tried to liberalize and democratize its system, Soviet tanks rolled in.

Elena was in Paris, France, visiting relatives (after receiving special permission to do so), when the invasion occurred. Returning to Moscow, she found the intellectual community more depressed and afraid than ever. She, like her future husband, would attend many trials and stand on many courtroom steps, supporting fellow dissidents.

Then, in June of 1970, a good friend and poet, Edward Kuznetsov, attempted to hijack a plane to draw attention to the plight of Jews wishing to emigrate. He was sentenced to death, along with his co-conspirators. Elena organized his defense, publicizing his case to Western journalists. She would later testify at his trial. His sentence was commuted to fifteen years in prison.

This was her first "official" dissent. In October, she would meet Andrei Sakharov. Together, they would continue the struggle for justice.

CHAPTER EIGHT

Détente and Human Rights

Détente. In French, it means "relaxation." In the language of foreign relations, it refers to the easing of tensions and moves toward cooperation between two countries, namely the United States and the Soviet Union. It is a concept and policy in many ways difficult to define. It has been used by different political groups in this country, and by the Soviet Union itself, to advance their own sometimes selfish points of view. An understanding of the attempts made to achieve détente, and the methods used, is, however, essential to the discussion of human rights.

During the Cold War, the period directly following World War II, the relationship between the United States and the Soviet Union could hardly have been worse. Between then and the official era of détente in the 1970s, occasional attempts had been made to lessen the animosity between the two superpowers. When General Secretary Khrushchev visited the United States in the late 1950s, at the same time "thawing" his own country, there had been hope that a cooperative relationship could be achieved. Again, in 1961, he met President Kennedy in Vienna. But two belligerent moves by the Soviet Union put a stop to any American efforts toward relaxation: the Cuban missile crisis, during which Khrushchev tried to establish a nuclear weapons base in Cuba, and the building of the Berlin Wall, effectively and symbolically dividing Europe into two camps, one a fortress of Soviet domination.

President Kennedy's assassination in 1963 and Khrushchev's ouster in 1964 halted almost all communication between the upper strata of government until the new leaders of both countries had time to decide on a foreign policy.

In addition, the United States was busy with intense problems of its own in the mid-1960s. It was all the new president, Lyndon Johnson, could do to handle them. There were riots throughout the country as the black civil rights movement swept the land. And America was waging an expensive and unpopular war in Vietnam. This war would claim the attention of foreign policy experts, cost billions of dollars, and set the American people against one another and against their own government.

But the Soviet Union and the United States could not put their relationship on the back burner for very long. The Soviet Union, whose economy was in dreadful shape, needed Western technology and trade to revitalize it. The United States, because of the rise of Soviet influence in Third World countries and primarily because of the quagmire of Vietnam, was no longer certain of its absolute supremacy in the world, economically or militarily. And, most of all, the arms race remained the biggest threat known to man. The faster the race became, the greater the danger. An agreement limiting and controlling these weapons had to be reached between the two major military powers in the world.

The Era of Détente

In some ways, it is ironic that President Richard Nixon was the person largely responsible for initiating a spirit of cooperation with the Soviet Union. His political career had begun at the height of the Cold War, when Nixon served first as senator from California, then as President Eisenhower's vice-president. He had vigorously opposed dealing with Russia with anything but military might. But it was now a decade later, and the previous ten years had seen both advances and setbacks in U. S.-Soviet relations. The setbacks themselves may have, in fact, led both parties to the bargaining table as each saw the other's strengths and weaknesses. Between 1969, when Nixon became president, and his resignation from office after the Watergate scandal in 1973, relations between the two superpowers took a turn toward understanding and co-existence. The first major arms control agreement, known as SALT I, was signed by both countries in 1972. Trade restrictions were loosened. There seemed a chance that progress was indeed being made, progress much like what Andrei Sakharov had proposed a few years earlier.

According to the memoirs of Henry Kissinger, President Nixon's secretary of state, there were two basic premises on which Nixon's policy toward the Soviet Union would be based. One was the concept of *containment*—making sure that the Soviet Union did not gain any more territory in the world, physically or politically. The second was the goal of peaceful co-existence and cooperation. One goal could not be realized without the other, and both depended on America's military and political strength. Kissinger was convinced, as was the

President Richard M. Nixon and Soviet leader Leonid Brezhnev signing an historic economic agreement. The period of détente was at its peak. *(Courtesy AP/Wide World Photos)*

president, that détente had to take place on America's terms. The Soviet Union could not be allowed to take advantage of the benefits of this policy while pursuing its own policy of domination, taking control of countries around the world against the will of the majority of their citizens.

When the Nixon administration took office in 1969, the Soviet Union had just invaded Czechoslovakia. The superpower was lending enormous military support to North Vietnam. The war in the Middle East raged on, also supported by the Soviet Union, which showed no willingness to help end it. Nixon intended to put a price on his brand of détente, and that price would be the ceasing of this very kind of behavior.

Linkage

Many saw in détente the possibility of forcing the

Soviet Union to change the way it conducted its foreign policy. The idea was to make things attractive to the Soviets—trade, scientific, and technological information, etc.—conditional on good Soviet behavior around the world. In exchange for a trade agreement that would benefit the Soviet Union, for instance, the Soviet Union might promise to stop supplying weapons to a revolutionary movement in another country. This concept of offering cooperation in exhange for concessions in policy is referred to as "linkage."

Linkage had its foes. Some thought it hindered the all-important business of controlling nuclear weapons. Others thought it would confuse matters to the point where nothing could be accomplished. And others felt that the Soviet Union was bluffing when it agreed to demands made on it, that the whole policy of détente would benefit the Soviet Union far more than the United States.

But linkage remained a part of our foreign policy throughout the 1970s. We attempted to use the leverage of our wealth and knowledge to influence the Soviet Union's foreign policy and to make demands on arms control agreements.

In 1972, a new dimension to linkage was added. The late Senator Henry Jackson and Congressman Charles Vanik introduced a bill into Congress that would change the dimension of the discussion. Up until this point, the U.S., although publicly deploring the internal system of the Soviet Union, had only dealt directly with the country on matters of international security and economic affairs. We did not want the Soviet Union to interfere with our domestic policies, and we agreed not to interfere with theirs.

The Jackson-Vanik Amendment, however, changed that. In an effort to increase economic cooperation between the two countries, a new trade agreement had been drafted by the White House. In it, the Soviet Union was granted the status of Most Favored Nation (MFN). This status had been withdrawn from the Soviet Union during the Korean War. Trade had continued at an almost normal pace, but the Soviet Union wanted the status of MFN returned as a symbolic gesture of goodwill.

In the meantime, the Soviet Union had recently imposed a new "exit tax" on those Soviet Jews wishing to leave the country. Before leaving the Soviet Union, they were required to pay the government a substantial sum of money. Many of them could not afford the tax. Most felt it was simply another device to keep people in the country against their will.

When the trade agreement reached Congress, Senator Jackson and Representative Vanik pushed for linkage between the right of Soviet Jews to emigrate and the bestowal of MFN status in the trade agreement. If the Soviet Union would promise to abolish the exit tax, then MFN status would remain part of the agreement. If not, it would be taken out. This was the first time that a foreign human rights issue became part of our foreign policy.

Again, Americans were divided over the issue. Some felt that insisting on internal changes would be seen by Moscow as a challenge to its sovereignty as a nation. If the Soviets gave in, therefore, they would appear weak in the eyes of the world. And the Soviet Union had proven time and again that under no circumstances would they risk appearing weak. Quiet diplomacy—careful, private negotiation—between high levels of government could achieve more than public moves with risky political strings attached.

Others, however, felt that the democratic traditions upon which America was founded, and for which it stood throughout the world, made it necessary for the United

States to consider human rights a part of its foreign policy. Along with our strength went a responsibility to all men and women, regardless of national boundaries. If we could use our power to make life more just for the Soviet people, we should. If the Soviet leadership refused to lighten its repressive load, then it should not receive the trade, economic, cultural, or other benefits of détente.

Andrei Sakharov on Détente

In a number of essential ways, Andrei Sakharov's concept of peaceful co-existence fit nicely inside the hopes Americans and Soviets had for the policy of détente. Scientific and cultural exchange could begin, and the threat of nuclear war would be diminished. The more we got to know one another, the more chances for a mixture of the best of both systems would improve.

On the other hand, Sakharov had spent the years from 1968 to 1973 looking more intensely at the problems within his own country. Human rights, freedom of speech, and the right to travel were all still denied his people. They had no intellectual freedom. He knew that none of his higher goals could be achieved without the essential liberalization and democratization occurring in his own country. And he saw no attempts being made by his government to begin this process on their own.

Sakharov called Western reporters to his apartment in Moscow on August 21, 1973, the fifth anniversary of the Soviet occupation of Czechoslovakia, to issue a statement on the process of détente:

Détente without democratization, détente in which the West in effect accepts the Soviet rules of the game, would be dangerous, it would not really solve any of the world's problems and would simply mean capitulation in the face of real or exaggerated Soviet power. It would mean trading with the Soviet Union, buying its gas and oil while ignoring other aspects. . . . I think if détente were to proceed totally without qualification on Soviet terms, it would pose a serious threat to the world as a whole. It would mean cultivating a closed country where anything that happens may be shielded from outside eyes, a country wearing a mask that hides its true face.

Indeed, Sakharov was becoming more and more appalled at the injustice and inefficiency of the Soviet system of government. His support for the ideal of socialism, his trust that the system could change, was weakening. On July 3, 1973, he had granted an interview to Olle Stenholm, a Swedish correspondent. During this interview, he expressed his growing dismay at what he saw around him. Lack of freedom was again his main complaint. But also, he said, there was astounding inequality between Soviet citizens in terms of access to food, consumer goods, and housing. Those who lived in the cities, for instance, had much more opportunity to eat well than those in the country. But worst of all, there was the illegal system of privilege for the Soviet elite, which he himself knew so well from his days in the weapons program. He went on to criticize the educational and medical systems, which he felt were poorly run.

For the first time, Sakharov expressed his own dissatisfaction with the idea of socialism as a whole. He felt that it showed more destructive features than positive ones. He was not a socialist, a Marxist, or a communist. He defined himself, in another interview, with Jay Axelbank of *Newsweek,* as a liberal.

In September of 1973, he wrote a letter to the United States Congress, urging them to enforce the Jackson-

Vanik Amendment. In this letter, he stressed that the right to choose one's country of residence was a right guaranteed by international law. He denied that linking human rights to international relations hindered negotiations, or that it represented interference in Soviet internal affairs. Instead, he insisted that the Jackson-Vanik Amendment was a protection of the rights of man, which superceded any national interests.

The Jackson-Vanik Amendment passed. The Soviet Union did withdraw the exit tax (after insisting that it had been applied mistakenly) and then received MFN status. But the true success or failure of linkage and, indeed, of the whole policy of détente practiced throughout the 1970s, is still being debated by political analysts on both sides.

Jimmy Carter and the Policy of Human Rights

When Jimmy Carter entered the White House in 1977, he put human rights at the top of his agenda. He vowed to carefully consider human rights in every country, communist or noncommunist, while deciding matters of foreign policy. This was the concept of linkage expressed in a very different way. He would condemn human rights violations conducted by our allies and made statements to that effect about abuses in Chile, Argentina, Uruguay, and other countries. It was his intent to make human rights a global, humanistic goal. In this way, human rights could be seen as the great strength of Western democracies throughout the world.

It was a noble and moral stance. As a political policy, it may have been more harmful than helpful in dealing with the Soviet Union. Although Carter insisted that he would condemn abuses wherever he found them, the Soviet

President Jimmy Carter, shaking the hand of Alejandro Orfila, the Secretary General of the Organization of American States, after signing the American Convention of Human Rights, June 1977. *(Courtesy AP/Wide World Photos)*

Union took his firm stance as a challenge. Restrictions on dissent in the Soviet Union increased, and tension between the two superpowers mounted.

But Jimmy Carter did have one supporter in Russia. On his inauguration day, Andrei Sakharov wrote a letter to the new president, urging him to continue to recognize human rights as an essential issue of the day. He also listed names of fifteen Soviet dissidents suffering in Soviet prisons for their actions, asking the president to remember them when making policy. President Carter replied to his letter, promising to keep working for the cause and commending Sakharov for his own courage. This exchange of letters was highly publicized, further infuriating the Soviet leaders.

Sakharov continued to praise Carter's efforts. In a 1978 article written for *Trialogue*, the magazine of the Trilateral Commission, a nonprofit, nongovernmental organization of private citizens seeking to foster closer cooperation among the regions of Western Europe, Japan, and North America, he wrote:

> I believe that President Carter's principled position responds to the demands of our time and to the democratic traditions of the American people. . . . I consider it very important that the principled position put forth by the United States Administration regarding the defense of human rights receive even broader support . . . in order for the U.S. to successfully carry out its leadership role in the Western world, to counterbalance the offensive policy of totalitarianism.

It is hard at this time to judge the whole effect of Carter's Human Rights Policy, except to say that it is largely through the international attention it received that human rights remains an integral part of foreign relations today.

CHAPTER NINE

The Nobel Prize

S uffering is even more intolerable when a victim knows that he is forgotten, that nobody in the world cares about his pain and destruction." Valery Chalidze, a dissident who had helped Andrei Sakharov form the Moscow Human Rights Committee in 1972, made that remark to Piero Ostellino, an Italian correspondent. In this spirit, and quite apart from official government efforts, there exists a number of independent human rights organizations around the world. These groups have no official political orientation or ideology; their purpose is to continually focus worldwide attention on human rights violations wherever and whenever they take place. The groups include Amnesty International, the International League for Human Rights, Freedom House, the Committee for Concerned Scientists, the Helsinki Watch Groups, and many others.

It is upon one document, almost without exception, that these organizations base their ideas on human rights: the United Nations Universal Declaration of Human Rights. It was developed in 1947 and adopted by the U.N. General Assembly, including the Soviet Union, in 1948. The declaration insists that the nations agreeing to it uphold the principles of human rights it expresses. These include freedom of speech and freedom to travel— freedoms that the civilized, modern people of the twentieth century consider fundamental, basic rights that all people deserve. It is this document that Andrei Sakharov has quoted and insisted that the Soviet Union live up to in dealing with its own population.

In 1975, a group of thirty–five nations, including the Soviet Union and the United States, met in Helsinki, Finland, for a conference concerning international security. These countries developed a very complicated, but essential document, called the Helsinki Final Act. The act places very strict limits on international and, in fact, internal behavior of the signatory nations, including proper treatment of prisoners, freedom of speech and assembly, respect for the sovereignty of national borders and a nation's right to self-determination, and many other rules of political and human rights behavior. The international economic and military accords put forth in this document remain as controversial as the policy of détente, and the results are just as inconclusive.

The human rights issue, however, was clarified as it had never been before. Very specific rules about how individuals were to be treated in any society were set down, and these rules closely resembled the U.N. declaration adopted back in 1948. The Soviet Union signed the Helsinki Act, knowing that the issue of human rights was now, more that ever, an international one. By signing the document, the Soviet leadership made promises other nations and individuals would try hard to hold them to.

In response to the signing of this agreement, for instance, the Moscow-Helsinki Watch Group was formed by Soviet dissidents who intended to monitor human rights violations in their country, using the Helsinki Accords as the basic guideline. Now crimes committed by

Soviet regimes had organized witnesses who did everything they could to see that violations were reported in
the international press. Branches were formed in other
Eastern bloc countries. The attempt was a noble one, but
with it came the inevitable retribution. Its founder, Yuri
Orlov, a physicist, was later arrested, and most other
members have also been silenced. Elena Bonner-
Sakharov herself is a member and she too has been
punished for her activities, which included countless
attempts, many successful, to publicize her husband's
case to the international press.

Another important human rights activity had been
conceived in 1974 by Andrei Sakharov and fellow dissidents after colleague Alexander Solzhenitsyn was expelled from the Soviet Union. The International
Sakharov Hearings were first held in Copenhagen, Den-
mark, in 1975. A number of people who had lived most of
their lives in the Soviet Union, but were now exiles or
emigrés, provided testimony concerning life in the East;
economic, physical, educational, and political conditions
were described in detail. A group of prominent human
rights scholars and Western civic leaders carefully ques-
tioned each witness to give the Western world a true
picture of what was happening in the Soviet Union.
Sakharov, in his personal letter to the first hearing, which
he was not allowed to attend, wrote,

I regard this [hearing being named after me] as a
recognition not only of my own personal merits, but
also as a recognition of all those in my country who
strive for full publicity, for the realization of human
rights, and especially for all those whose loss of freedom is the high price they pay for these endeavors. I am
sure that the witnesses of this hearing, on the basis of
numerous documents and their personal experiences,

will be able to present a convincing picture of the ways in which people are persecuted—both within and outside the process of law.

Indeed, witnesses and experts flocked to this conference, and the two others that followed in 1977 and 1979. Their stories of pain and hardship were highly publicized in the West, and a clearer picture did emerge of life in the Eastern bloc countries. But these witnesses were, in many ways, the lucky ones. They had survived their experiences and were free to tell the world about them. Others, the ones they hoped to help with their difficult reminiscences, were still in prisons or psychiatric hospitals or exile or, like Sakharov himself, simply denied the right to leave the country to attend the conference personally.

The Nobel Prize

While the first Sakharov Hearing was being organized, another international organization was considering Andrei Sakharov for an honor of its own. The Nobel Committee, in Oslo, Norway, had decided to give Dr. Sakharov its highest award: the Nobel Prize for Peace. Another winner of the prize had been Martin Luther King, Jr., for his work as the leader of the black civil rights movement in the United States. (Future winners would include Amnesty International, as a group, for its courageous struggle to release political prisoners throughout the world; and Jimmy Carter, who would share the prize with Menachem Begin of Israel and Anwar Sadat of Egypt for the signing of the Camp David Agreement on peace between the two Middle Eastern countries.)

In awarding the Nobel Peace Prize to Andrei Sakharov in 1975, the committee cited his "personal and fearless effort in the cause of peace among mankind" and his "message of peace and justice to all peoples in the world. For him, it is a fundamental principle that world peace can have no lasting value unless it is founded on respect for the individual human being in society."

To Sakharov, the prize represented two things. It was not only a great honor to him, but also to the entire fight for human rights being waged by so many courageous people in his country. Although again he was not allowed to leave the country, his wife Elena made the trip to Oslo. In accepting the prize for her husband, she delivered a moving and impassioned speech, entitled "Peace, Progress and Human Rights," which repeated Sakharov's messages of warning and hope.

Another Soviet, who by that time had been expelled from his country for writing and publishing "anti-Soviet slander" in the West, would be awarded the Nobel Prize for Literature in 1980. His name is Alexander Solzhenitsyn, and he is, perhaps, even more famous than Sakharov in the West for his brave, dissident voice.

As an author, his works stand among those of the great writers of the twentieth century. But it is his subject matter, the brutal labor camps and hospitals in which he himself spent many years during Stalin's Reign of Terror, that claimed the attention of the world. His books, namely the three volumes of *The Gulag Archipelago,* exposed the crimes of Stalin in the cold light of the 1960s and 1970s. During the Khrushchev Thaw it had been tolerated, but as the Brezhnev era proceeded, his outcries became more offensive to the authoritics until, in 1974, they expelled him from his homeland, against his will.

Solzhenitsyn and Division Among Dissidents

In appearance, Sakharov and Solzhenitsyn could not be more dissimilar. Solzhenitsyn is a "typical" Russian in

Sakharov and his mother-in-law, Ruf Bonner, hearing the news that Sakharov had won the Nobel Peace Prize, October 9, 1975. *(Courtesy Efrem Yankelevich)*

figure—large, blustering, with a full beard and ruddy complexion. Sakharov, on the other hand, is tall and rather frail, and his pale complexion is set off by white, thinning hair. While Solzhenitsyn is aggressive in conversation, by all accounts Sakharov is more contemplative and quiet.

In their political philosophies, too, there are differences. Indeed, dissent in the Soviet Union takes many shapes and forms, perhaps as many as there are dissidents. It could be said, however, that there are three basic schools of thought as expressed by three renowned Soviet dissidents. But it must be stressed that their differences in thinking do not greatly affect their unity of opposition to the conditions in their country. The differences have more to do with how each sees the West and how best to tackle the problems confronting the Soviet Union.

Solzhenitsyn, for instance, sees the problems facing the Soviet Union and its people as the result of the modern age in general, as well as the Soviet system itself. It is his opinion that it is modern values, including some aspects of Western capitalism and democracy, that are to blame for the state in which mankind finds itself. He sees the greatest hope for his people in a return to a religious, centralized government—an authoritarian rule, without Soviet leadership or a socialist economy. The West cannot help the Soviet Union, in his view. Russia must concentrate on solving its own problems by returning to this religious, autocratic system.

Another dissident view, expressed by Roy Medvedev, Soviet historian and self-proclaimed socialist, also believes that the West cannot solve Russia's internal problems. Medvedev believes in the basic tenets of socialism, but struggles to do away with the harsh repressive measures his government enforces. He wishes to see democratic reform take place, resulting in a multiparty system, but still believes in the economic benefits of socialism for his country. He also thinks that the Soviet people cannot rely on Western pressure to relieve internal human rights violations. The West, he believes, has only so much influence on Soviet affairs. By necessity, the West must concentrate on the military security of the world rather than the Soviet internal situation. It is up to the Soviet people themselves to reform the system from within.

Andrei Sakharov represents yet another point of view. Although once a believer in socialism, he has now, as we've seen, turned away from it. He sees in Western democracy the greatest hope for a life of freedom for the individual and also believes that Western attention and pressure represents the greatest chance for reform in his country. Yet his is not essentially a political struggle— capitalism against socialism or the United States against the Soviet Union. It is, instead, a humanitarian effort, based on the wider question of basic human rights for his

Soviet author and exile, Alexander Solzhenitsyn. *(Courtesy AP/Wide World Photos)*

people and for all mankind. Without these rights and freedoms, nothing else of long-lasting value can be accomplished.

While there are rather strong disagreements between these men on specific ideas, they do stand together in equal condemnation of the Soviet Union and its practice of repression. Their names have appeared on many of the same petitions protesting human rights violations, and on letters supporting each other's right to speak out.

Each in his own way has also been the subject of harassment by his government for his activities. Roy Medvedev, still living in Moscow, has been under constant KGB surveillance for years. Alexander Solzhenitsyn was expelled from his country and denied his citizenship.

Andrei Sakharov is now in exile in the city of Gorki after more than ten years of constant harassment. His case is unique among all other dissidents. This uniqueness has not only saved his life and allowed him to speak out more than most, but is probably what has him trapped inside the Soviet Union, perhaps forever. It is his stature as a scientist, as the "father of the Soviet hydrogen bomb," and his years of service to the state before 1968, that has kept him relatively safe. But his former access to the inner workings of the Soviet military complex—and its military secrets—during those years has provided the Soviet authorities with an excellent excuse to keep him inside the country, helpless now in Gorki, and silent.

CHAPTER TEN

The Road to Gorki

The road to exile for Andrei Sakharov was, it is true, a longer one than for most who speak out. He had been able, for nearly fifteen years, to wage his fight for freedom and dignity in the Soviet Union. Others, not as well known and respected throughout the world, would suffer harsh sentences in prisons, psychiatric hospitals, and exile, with only a few like Sakharov to speak out for them. For many reasons, the State felt it could not risk the international outrage it would incite if serious action were taken against Sakharov. This attitude would, over the years, and for many other reasons, change. And, while Sakharov himself remained relatively safe, he and those close to him would be slowly, methodically harassed in painful, sometimes cruel ways.

The years after the publication of "Thoughts on Progress," 1968 to 1973, were more or less quiet ones in terms of pressure on Sakharov from the authorities. He did lose all security clearance for his military work and the benefits that came with it, including precious access to the inner workings of the Soviet system. On the other hand, as he told Jay Axelbank of *Newsweek* in 1972, "nobody bothers me except when the KGB follow me every once in awhile."

But the pressure began to mount. On September 6, 1972, Sakharov took part in a demonstration in front of the Lebanese Embassy in Moscow, protesting the killing of Israeli athletes during the Munich Olympics by Palestinian terrorists. He was detained, though not arrested, by regular police. Then, shortly after that incident, both his stepdaughter Tatyana and stepson Alexei were expelled from the schools they had been attending. His wife Elena was called in by the KGB to explain her "activities," including the help she was giving to Edward Kuznetsov, in prison for the hijacking attempt in Leningrad. Clearly, the authorities were taking notice of Sakharov's own activities, which had been steadily increasing.

Then an extraordinary trial of two dissidents took place in August and September of 1973. Peter Yakir and Victor Krasin had been arrested for anti-Soviet activities that summer. Unlike most dissidents, they had broken down under the pressure of KGB interrogation, naming others in the movement and denouncing their actions. It was reported that Sakharov had met Yakir on several occasions, and that Sakharov's material had been used by Yakir and Krasin in their own "anti-Soviet propaganda." This linked Sakharov quite specifically to convicted "slanderers," a fact that would be used by the KGB frequently.

Sakharov later gave an interview to a Dutch radio station, by telephone, about the trial and the two men who had cooperated with the KGB. "I am sad. These people have been broken. I have never been in their situation, and I do not presume to judge them. . . . I know that Yakir had a difficult life. . . . After the arrest of his own father, he spent eighteen years behind bars. He grew up in absolutely inhuman surroundings. After that, I cannot accuse him of anything. I pity him and I pity his family." Then, two months after Sakharov had petitioned the head of the KGB to release a former mathematics teacher who had been charged with "anti-Soviet slander," the first of the press campaigns against Sakharov took place.

The Press Campaign

Since nearly all information the Soviet people receive is what their government prints in newspapers and broadcasts on radio and television, a press campaign against a citizen can be quite effective. Western radio, like "Voice of America" and other broadcasts, can sometimes get through the sophisticated jamming devices set up by the Soviet government. For the most part, however, the average citizen receives no information other than what the government gives to him. The dangerous, underground world of *samizdat* and dissent does not, for obvious reasons, appeal to many people living in that fear-ridden country.

In the summer and fall of 1973, the Soviet people were given a rather startling picture of Andrei Sakharov in the press. For many, it would be their first introduction to him. They had perhaps heard of this great scientist, but knew no details about his life or his opinions. He was, however, beginning to create a stir, internally and internationally, and the Soviet leadership had to put a stop to it the best way they could. Partially to offset any influence he might have on his own people should some of his opinions reach their ears, and mostly to frighten and discredit him and fellow dissidents, the authorities made full use of the press they strictly controlled.

In this first campaign, they focused mostly on his recent statements concerning détente and, of course, his constant defense of those people the Soviet state referred to as slanderers. In newspapers and on radio, they called him a traitor and accused him of slander and of defending "anti-Soviet elements." They accused him of trying to undermine the Soviet's good efforts to proceed with détente, and of being controlled and used by "hostile Western propaganda."

Perhaps worst of all, the KGB had forty members of the esteemed Academy of Sciences, Sakharov's colleagues in the organization to which he still belongs, sign a letter denouncing him. It was not the first time that this tactic had been used, nor would it be the last for Sakharov. In a way, it is hard to understand why the very citizen whose rights Sakharov was fighting to protect would want to help bring about his downfall. Dr. Valentin Turchin, in an interview with Hedrick Smith, explained it this way: "The honest man makes the silent one feel guilty for not having spoken out. They cannot understand how he had the courage to do what they could not bring themselves to do. So they feel impelled to speak out against him to protect their own consciences."

This first campaign was abruptly stopped in September, mainly as a result of protests from Western leaders. Perhaps most important was a telegram from Philip Handler, President of the American Academy of Sciences, to his counterpart in the Soviet Academy of Sciences warning that if harassment of Sakharov was not stopped, "it would have severe effects upon relationships between the scientific communities of the U.S. and the U.S.S.R. and could [impair] our recent efforts toward increasing interchange and cooperation."

Later, in another massive press campaign in 1983, and in constant press releases in between, Sakharov would again be referred to as a traitor and slanderer. Scientists would again be called to denounce him and, in 1983, over 2,400 Soviet people—average citizens—would write horrible, vicious letters to the Sakharovs, already in exile in Gorki, in response to articles in the Soviet press. As the years passed, the press would not only focus their attacks on Dr. Sakharov, but on his wife as well. Elena was an evil influence on him, claimed the press. She, as well as hostile Western forces, was using him and distorting his views for her own selfish purposes. These reports against her frequently referred to the fact that she was half Jewish, playing upon the anti-Semitic, racist attitudes of some, though certainly not all, Soviet people.

But the press could work *for* Sakharov as well as against him—if it were the foreign press. For until his exile to Gorki and even after, with the help of his wife, Sakharov used his access to foreign journalists to counteract false accusations and clarify his misrepresented opinions, and continue to report any and all human rights violations the Soviets continued to deny. The foreign press was not controlled by the whims of the Soviet government. They were allowed to print whatever they could find out in this secretive country. And find out they did, mainly through the courageous efforts of Sakharov and his wife.

Nineteen seventy-three was a hard year for dissidents, one of the hardest since Khrushchev had been ousted. It was in 1973 that Sakharov was called in to see the KGB, for the first in a long series of "interviews and interrogations."

The Sakharovs and the KGB

Sakharov's first interview took place a few months before the press campaign, on March 23. He was told that he was not "morally sound" and that his membership in the Moscow Human Rights Committee was "slander" against the Soviet Union. The very existence of such a committee implied that there was a human rights problem, which defamed the "perfect Soviet state." He was advised that the Western press was using him to destroy détente so that they could continue their arms race and take over the Soviet Union. While he was not told directly to stop his dissident activities, the threat of further harassment if he continued was made clear.

A second interview took place in early August, with a high-ranking officer named Michail Malyrov. Sakharov would later recount this entire conversation from memory to Western journalists on August 18. This second interview was prompted, many think, by the interview he had given in July to Swedish correspondent Olle Stenholm, which has been quoted here in some detail. Sakharov himself has said that it was the Stenholm interview, in which he first expressed his disillusionment with socialism and described in detail some of the desperate conditions in the Soviet Union, that was the "straw that broke the camel's back."

The Soviet leadership would not stand much more from this scientist, once the receiver of so many privileges and honors from the very state he was now condemning. He was meddling in foreign affairs and internal politics, so highly protected by an insecure, yet extremely powerful, ruling body. They could not afford to have their citizens questioning how things were run in this massive country, especially not one as renowned throughout the world as Andrei Sakharov.

Things were to get much worse for him and his family. Later in 1973, two men claiming to be members of a Palestinian organization, Black September, broke into the Sakharov apartment and held the couple and Elena's son, Alexei, hostage for nearly two hours. The men cut the telephone wires and did not allow anyone to answer the door. They accused Sakharov of being "under the influence" of his Jewish wife when speaking out against Palestinian tactics in the recent Arab-Israeli conflict in the Middle East. They demanded he change his views. They told the family that they would not kill them, but that there were worse things that could happen, and abruptly left.

By all objective accounts, it is highly unlikely that these men were indeed Arab terrorists. In a closed society, and especially considering that Andrei Sakharov had been so closely watched by the KGB, it would be virtually impossible for the authorities to be unaware of the visit. As shocking as it may seem, many consider this another way of trying to frighten the Sakharovs into silence. It did not work. Andrei Sakharov continued to write, give interviews to the Western press, and attend the trials of other dissidents. These trials were also becoming more and more dangerous for him.

In 1976, a major confrontation with the police occurred at the trial of a Crimean Tatar, R. Dzhemilev, who had spoken out for the right of his people to reestablish their homeland. There would be some violence at this encounter—a shoving match between the Sakharovs and the police when the Sakharovs were denied access to the courtroom and physically harassed. They were then detained and fined for their activities. Then in 1978, at another trial, this time of the courageous founder of the Moscow-Helsinki Watch Group, Yuri Orlov, a similar incident took place. The Sakharovs were detained overnight and again fined. Tension was continuing to mount and Sakharov, perhaps for the first time, was beginning to feel afraid, not for himself, but for his family.

The Family

In 1973 alone, Elena was subjected to at least three

interrogations by the KGB. She and her family had become the major target of Soviet pressure. Unable, because of international attention, to really harm Sakharov himself, the KGB worked on those he loved most.

Indeed, Ruf Bonner, who herself had spent seventeen grueling years in Stalin's gulag, told reporter Kevin Klose in 1982, "For me, there was nothing left to be afraid of. Yet even I was afraid . . . from the moment Sakharov appeared in our lives. I who had been through the camps also, was afraid again. So I understand the power of fear. . . . I can't judge others if I myself was afraid." She was afraid with good reason. By the middle of 1978, she would see her grandchildren and great-grandchildren leave the Soviet Union forever. Only she and her grandson's fiancée, Liza, remained behind to support her daughter and son-in-law.

After being expelled from school in 1973, Tatyana and Alexei, Elena's children, had been under constant pressure and surveillance. They were used as weapons against their stepfather and were unable to lead normal lives in their own country. Given a choice of remaining in the Soviet Union to be further harassed, perhaps internally exiled, and used against their parents, the children made the difficult decision to leave the country. Tatyana, her husband Efrem Yankelevich, and their children left first, in late 1977. Alexei, after receiving promises from the authorities that his fiancée, Liza Alexeyeva, would be able to join him in the United States, left on March 1, 1978. The Bonner-Sakharovs were slowly being isolated from everyone close to them.

There was hardly anyone left for them in the Soviet Union. Almost all of the other dissident voices had been silenced in one way or another in the past years. Solzhenitsyn had been expelled. Zhores Medvedev, Valentin

Turchin, and Valery Chalidze joined him, by force, in the West. Hundreds of others, famous and unknown, were in prisons, psychiatric hospitals, or exiled in the Soviet Union, unable to speak out. Only a few voices could still be heard. One belonged to Andrei Sakharov.

But for him, and for the world at large, the difficult, perhaps fruitless attempts at reform and cooperation, within and outside of the Soviet Union, ended abruptly in 1979. When Soviet tanks rolled into the Asian country of Afghanistan to subdue a revolution and install a government more to their liking, the world was shocked. This act represented a blatant disregard for every principle embodied in détente, in the Helsinki Accords, and in all other security agreements.

The outrage at the illegality of the act was expressed eloquently by Andrei Sakharov in a powerful statement to the Western press shortly after the invasion. Three weeks later, the KGB would arrest him, strip him of all awards and honors, and send him to Gorki.

CHAPTER ELEVEN

Gorki

I live in an apartment guarded night and day by a policeman at the entrance. He allows no one to enter but family members. . . . I am unable to telephone Moscow or Leningrad, even from the public telephone at the post office. The call is immediately disconnected at the order of the KGB agents who always follow me. I receive very little mail, and that consists mainly of letters "re-educating" me or merely cursing me.

When I accompanied my mother-in-law [Ruf Bonner] to the station on her departure for Moscow, KGB agents, pistols in hand, made a show of preventing me from approaching the coach, making it clear that the order forbidding me from going beyond the city limits was not just empty words. . . . While we are out walking the KGB agents are in our apartment damaging the typewriter and tape recorder or searching through our papers. . . .

This article is being taken to Moscow by my wife, my constant helper, who shares my exile and willingly takes upon herself the heavy burden of traveling back and forth, handling my communications with the outside world, coping with the growing hatred of the KGB.

Earlier she withstood the poison of slander and insinuation, focused more on her than me. The fact that I am Russian and my wife is half Jewish has proven useful for the internal purposes of the KGB. . . . In terms of everyday life, my situation is much better than that of my friends sent into exile or sentenced to labor camp or prison. But all the measures taken against me have not a shred of legality. It is part of a harsh, nationwide campaign against dissidents, including the attempt to force me to keep silent and thereby make it easier for repressive action against others. . . . It is impossible to foresee what awaits us. Our only protection is the spotlight of public attention on our fate by friends around the world. . . .

The above was written by Sakharov in May of 1980, when conditions, as bad as they were, were better than they are now. At this writing (April 1985), the Sakharovs have not been seen by any friend or objective reporter (only the KGB) since May 6, 1984. Their children and grandchildren living in Newton, Massachusetts, have received postcards from them every few months, stating simply that they are alive and well, and telling them not to worry. But, of course, they do worry. It has been a hard five years of worrying, and waiting to see what will happen next.

The First Year

From the beginning, Andrei Sakharov's exile was illegal, even by Soviet standards. He had no trial, was never charged with a specific crime, has never known his accusers. Sakharov wasted no time after being exiled to communicate the illegality of his plight to the world. And the world responded—telegrams and letters from nearly every official Western government office and organization were sent to the Soviet leadership. Each and every one protested against the inhuman situation in which the Sakharovs had been placed. The international scientific community joined in the protest. Members of the Committee for Concerned Scientists, who have kept a constant watch on the Sakharovs, signed a petition to the Soviet Academy of Sciences, calling upon it to take some positive action on behalf of one of their most esteemed members. The New York Academy of Science, as well as scientific counterparts all over the world, joined in. Cries of outrage from human rights organizations all over the world were voiced.

But these protests, and the ones that were to follow throughout the next years, fell upon seemingly deaf ears. While we probably will never know who finally decided to send Sakharov to Gorki, we do know that any decision once made in the Soviet Union is rarely reversed, especially in a case so highly publicized. At the time the decision was reached, the authorities probably felt two things: that Sakharov had gone too far when he criticized the Soviet invasion of Afghanistan; the government certainly did not need one of its most famous citizens adding his condemnation to that of nearly the entire Western world. At the same time, they had nothing to lose because of that very international condemnation. Détente was finished. The era of cooperation, real or imagined, was over. They could now ignore the West's outrage and finally silence a man who had embarrassed them for over ten years. Not only had he spoken out against the shortcomings of the Soviet economy and internal conditions, but he had intruded into foreign affairs, with his philosophy of "peaceful co-existence" as the only way to peace. Worst of all, he had publicized the trials and sentences of Soviet dissidents to a Western press eager to print such long-hidden and denied information.

A rare photograph of Sakharov in exile, Gorki, 1982. *(Courtesy Efrem Yankelevich)*

And silence him they have. But it took more than merely exiling him to Gorki. For, until May of 1984, he and his wife continued their struggle for justice—for others and, out of necessity, for themselves and those close to them.

The Battle For Liza

"I consider that the defense of our children is as legitimate as that of other victims of injustice, but in this case, it appears that it was precisely myself and my activities that were the cause of human suffering." Andrei Sakharov was referring to the case of Liza Alexeyeva, his future daughter-in-law, who was being held against her will in the Soviet Union, because she had had the misfortune to fall in love with Sakharov's stepson. After nearly four years of begging the authorities, Liza was still unable to leave the country and join Alexei in the United

States. She was depressed and full of despair. It seemed hopeless.

Liza herself had committed no crime, not even in Soviet terms. She had never been a dissident and was only twenty years old when she met young Alexei, himself just twenty-one. They were students together at the Lenin Pedagogical Institute (a teachers' college) when they fell in love. Alexei tried to keep her from becoming involved in his family's activities, knowing all too well how thoroughly the KGB could destroy a life even slightly involved with Sakharov. But when it was time for him to leave the Soviet Union, she was not allowed to go with him. Promises were made that when her visa was in order, she could join him. But it was now 1981, and the promises had not been kept.

Only Liza and Ruf Bonner, Elena's mother, remained behind when the Bonner-Sakharov children, son-in-law Efrem Yankelevich, and grandchildren departed. Ruf later had been given permission to leave, while Liza had been denied it—part of Soviet strength lies in its unpredictability. Ruf refused to leave without Liza. The two of them stayed in the Bonner-Sakharov apartment in Moscow, once home to Andrei, Elena, and the rest of the family. They traveled to Gorki when they were allowed, continued to appeal for Liza's exit visa, and helped Elena when she came to Moscow.

The apartment itself was under constant KGB guard. No one came or left without being watched, sometimes harassed. But Elena's trips were very fruitful. She brought messages from Sakharov to Western journalists about his condition, family situation, and human rights violations he still learned of, even in Gorki. She tried to constantly bring worldwide attention to her husband's situation and his important opinions.

More and more, Sakharov concentrated on Liza's

plight. The injustice of it, and his partial responsibility for it, weighed heavily upon him and his wife. Every appeal to both Western and Soviet sources was ignored. It was time, the couple thought, to take matters more forcefully into their own hands. They would do battle with the Soviet authorities, and it would be a deadly test of wills.

The First Hunger Strike

On November 22, 1981, Andrei and Elena Sakharov stopped eating. Two months before, they had informed the world of their decision to embark upon a hunger strike if Liza were not allowed to go to the United States. They would not eat again until Liza and Alexei were together.

The hunger strike is a tricky political weapon. It has been used throughout history to bring attention to, and attempt to force action on, many different political and personal causes. Mahatma Gandhi used hunger strikes in his fight for India's independence from Britain, along with other nonviolent methods of protests. His methods, as a whole, were successful. Members of the Irish Republican Army, jailed in the Maze Prison for terrorist activities, used it in their struggle in Northern Ireland. Ten young men starved themselves to death and the war still rages on. Sakharov himself had fasted for eleven days during President Nixon's trip to Moscow in 1974. He wanted to bring attention to the plight of dissident poet Vladimir Bukovsky, who had recently been jailed. Bukovsky was later released.

It is sometimes hard to judge the effectiveness of a hunger strike. One cannot know, for instance, if Sakharov's hunger strike had any direct connection to Bukovsky's release three years later. This method of protest is almost always used as a last measure, to gain attention and give a time limit—the time it takes someone to starve to death—for action to be taken. Sakharov demanded that the attention of Western journalists focus on Bukovsky during Nixon's visit, and it was. That attention fixed his plight in the minds of millions of people in the world.

The immediate practical effects of a hunger strike can almost always be measured—the striker lives or dies, his demands are met or denied. But the symbolic effects are beyond measurement. No matter the reason for the strike, it is always painful and difficult for the world to watch as someone starves to death for his beliefs.

In this case, it would be the Sakharovs, two esteemed international figures in intellectual, scientific, and human rights circles. The strike's effect depended on the international spotlight that would surely be upon them; perhaps no other two people in the Soviet Union could attract this much attention. Their cause was their son's right to be with his fiancée, and the right of that couple—and any couple on the face of the earth—to choose their place of residence freely.

It was not an easy decision to make. Neither Sakharov nor Bonner were in particularly good health. They both suffered from chronic heart and circulatory problems— Sakharov himself had had a heart attack in 1973. Elena Bonner's eyesight had continued to be troublesome, requiring extensive treatment and surgery, which she had received outside of the Soviet Union, in Italy. Sakharov was now sixty years old, Elena Bonner fifty-eight. It took a hardy physical constitution to withstand the abuse a hunger strike inflicted, and neither of them had one.

But they were determined. Despite the pleadings of their friends and acquaintances, they insisted. By this time, Ruf had relented and gone to a new life in the United States. Liza had been forewarned about the strike and tried her best to understand that it was necessary. She had promised them she would support them, but found it extremely difficult. She would later tell Kevin Klose,

> [Their friends] were all worried, of course, about what the strike might do to Elena Georgievna and Andrei Dmitrievich, how they'd come out of it. This effort to persuade them not to go through with it added to the difficulty they faced. And I was trying to convince the friends that the decision was the right one. While all the time I myself was worrying about it no less than they. To tell the friends that the strike was necessary . . . inescapable . . . was terribly hard for me.

The strike began at midnight on November 22, 1981, with Elena Bonner and Sakharov together in Gorki. At the end of the first week, Sakharov managed to smuggle a letter out, in it stating that, "No change in our health or empty words will change our minds, only the departure of Liza. . . . A tragic end will signify a murder agreed to by the KGB and by the complete silence of my colleagues in the Academy of Sciences. . . . "

Indeed, the bugging and wiretapping of the Sakharov apartment gave the KGB a firsthand record of their deteriorating conditions. By the end of the first week, Sakharov had lost almost seventeen pounds, Elena Bonner nearly fifteen. Sakharov's blood pressure was falling. Yet no action was taken. The whole world was watching and protesting, but the Soviet government made no move to release Liza to the West. Another week passed. On the thirteenth day of the strike, the police in Gorki broke into the apartment and took the Sakharovs to two separate hospitals. KGB agents first informed Sakharov that his wife had given in and stopped the strike; he refused to believe them and continued his fast. Elena was then told that her husband was dying. She too refused to give up and vowed she would not eat until Liza was free.

Liza herself was in Moscow, denied the chance to go to Gorki to see and support her future in-laws. Instead, she tried her best to plead for her release to the authorities there. Finally, on the eighteenth day of the strike, with Elena almost in a coma and Sakharov steadily weakening, the authorities relented. Liza could go. After a tearful good-bye, the Sakharovs wished their last close relative well and sent her to the West.

The Sakharovs had won this test of wills. But they would not win all of their battles, and their lives would remain far from pleasant in the future.

More Harassment

Despite the heavy toll the hunger strike took on them, they were not ready to submit to silence. Their work would continue. Elena traveled back and forth from Moscow to Gorki, bringing news and supplies to Sakharov, and appeals and statements from him to the outside world. Western journalists, with Elena's encouragement, frequently gathered at the Moscow apartment for statements when she was in town. She worked hard, alone now that Liza and Ruf were in America.

Sakharov, too, was not idle. His scientific work developed as he continued to study the universe and its origins. Even in exile, he produced some extremely important papers, although he himself was not particularly pleased with his work. Years before, in 1973, he had told reporters at a press conference, ". . . I have not been satisfied with my productivity in scientific work. Two things have played decisive roles in this: first, the fact that, as theoretical physicists go, I am well along in years; second, the stressful—and recently very alarming—situation in which people close to me, my family, and I find ourselves." Although this statement applied even more to the early 1980s, he produced some stunning work. In 1980 and 1981, he was elected a foreign member of both the Italian and French Academies of Sciences.

It is, indeed, astounding that Sakharov could work at all under the conditions in which he and his wife lived. In addition to the everyday tension of living under constant guard, they were subjected to unexpected, cruel actions. One day in 1980, two men pretending to be workers who had had too much to drink, stormed their home. Swinging around pistols, they threatened the couple, called Sakharov "insane," and left. This time, as in 1973, the KGB certainly must have been aware of this visit and, if they were not responsible for setting it up, at least did nothing to stop it.

Dr. Sakharov's personal papers, which he carried

Sakharov in his home in Gorki, March 1984. (*Courtesy Efrem Yankelevich*)

around in a briefcase whenever he went out so that they would not be stolen by the KGB if left at home, were, despite his precautions, stolen from him at least three times. Once, while he was sitting in his car, two men smashed the car window and took the briefcase from the back seat. That time alone, he lost five hundred pages of typed material and nine hundred pages of handwritten notes, letters, and diaries.

Another press campaign was conducted, this one more vicious than any that had preceded it. Twenty-four hundred letters, from average citizens, were sent to Gorki, all cruel and angry. Members of the Academy of Sciences once again denounced their colleague. The couple could not walk down the streets of Gorki without being called traitors, slanderers, and worse. Once again, the ugly face of anti-Semitism was showing itself and Elena Bonner was forced to withstand this racism.

Then a ray of hope shone in the spring of 1982. There were rumors in Moscow that the Sakharovs would be allowed to emigrate. Universities in Norway and the United States immediately invited him to accept a teaching post at their institutions. Sakharov decided he was now willing to leave his homeland forever, something he had not really been able or willing to consider before. It looked as if there might be an end to this isolation and torture. But just as quickly as the suggestion of leaving was offered, it was taken away. No one knows why. The possibility of emigration has never been mentioned again.

The Second Hunger Strike and a Disappearance

The years of exile had put a tremendous strain on both Sakharovs. But, perhaps, even more pressure was felt by Elena. It was up to her to make the long journeys back and forth between Gorki and Moscow, to keep attention focused on her husband's plight, to run the constant risk of harassment by the KGB in Moscow as well as in Gorki. She was in contact with the American Embassy, hoping for some help from our diplomatic corps, and in constant communication with Western journalists.

This intense activity placed a strain on her health as well as her emotional life. Since 1979, she had not been allowed to travel to Italy, where she had received medical treatment for her failing eyesight. Despite petitions on her behalf from Sakharov and supporters in the West, the authorities refused to allow her to even temporarily leave the country. In 1983, she suffered one heart attack in April, another in October. Dr. Sakharov himself was unwell at the time, also suffering from a heart condition, but he was far more worried about his wife. He wrote in 1983, "I fear—and I believe the fear is justified—that if Elena were to be hospitalized some means may be found to bring about her death. The risk would be greater if she were alone, but it wouldn't be eliminated completely by my presence. . . . The only acceptable solution is for my wife to go abroad. This is the only way to save her life. . . ."

In early 1984, Sakharov decided, despite his own declining health, to go on another hunger strike, this time to make sure his wife received proper medical care. He issued a statement in April that pleaded with his scientific colleagues and public and government figures to help him now, "at this tragic moment of our life. . . . My hunger strike is of indefinite duration. I will end it only when my wife receives permisson to go abroad. Her death will be mine as well. Once again, as I did two years ago, I ask for your help. Save us!"

What actually happened after Dr. Sakharov's hunger strike began on May 2, no one can say for certain. On

May 6, a friend of the family managed to see the Sakharovs in Gorki. She found out that Elena had been charged with "defaming the Soviet state" and was restricted to Gorki. She would no longer be able to travel to Moscow and communicate on Sakharov's behalf to the outside world. The curtain of silence descended completely on the Sakharovs—their isolation was total. No one has seen them since.

From then on, only sketchy reports and educated guesses about their condition and whereabouts have been made. The Soviet government has continually issued statements claiming that they are both fine and working happily, but they have refused to allow anyone to see or speak with either of them.

During the summer of 1984, terrifying reports reached the West that Dr. Sakharov had been taken to a hospital in Gorki and was being treated by Dr. Vladimir Rozhnov, a Soviet psychiatrist, who was flown from Moscow to Gorki every other day to treat his star patient. A psychiatric source in Moscow confirmed the report about Dr. Rozhnov and stated that Sakharov was being given mind-altering drugs and/or hypnosis in an attempt to get him to renounce his human rights and political stands. Apparently he has remained strong enough to refuse, despite this cruel and inhuman method of repression.

In August, it was reported by a West German newspaper that Elena Bonner had indeed been sentenced to five years of internal exile. She had been arrested just before Sakharov's hunger strike began back in May, apparently on her way to seek political asylum in the American Embassy in Moscow. She was sentenced for breaking Article 190-1 of the Soviet Criminal Code that forbids "slander of the Soviet state and social system."

As far as anyone knows, the Sakharovs were rejoined in their Gorki apartment in early September of 1984 and

One of the latest pictures of Elena Bonner and Andrei Sakharov, taken in September 1984. *(Courtesy Efrem Yankelevich)*

have been living in Gorki, in complete isolation, ever since. A few photographs and even a videotape of them was released to the West. But neither the U.S. government nor the Bonner-Sakharov children here in the United States feel that these tapes, photographs, or scant postcards prove anything about the Sakharovs' true condition. Until an eyewitness reports that they are well, the Sakharovs' situation will remain a mystery.

The questions posed at the beginning of this book— What were their crimes? Who judged them guilty? And why?—have no definite answers. The crimes of Andrei Sakharov and Elena Bonner are not crimes as we understand them here in America. They have not hurt anyone, stolen anything, lied or cheated. Sakharov has only spoken out against a government that protects itself from anyone who disagrees with its methods. He has criticized that government in the eyes of the world—a world it fears and, in many ways, despises. Elena Bonner has defended the principles of justice and peace, and made the "mistake" of falling in love with the state's number one enemy, Andrei Sakharov. Who judged them guilty? There has been no court of law, no jury, no judge. It is the mammoth vehicle of repression that Stalin so forcefully installed in his country —and the people who now run that vehicle so mercilessly —that has made Sakharov and his fellow dissidents guilty of crimes against the state. No one human, no one bad law, can be held responsible.

Why has Sakharov been sent into exile? Why has Elena been sentenced with him? Why do others suffer in prisons and psychiatric hospitals? The answers to those questions are wrapped up in the long and tortuous history of this grand country, and in the huge bureaucracy of Soviet communism and imperialism.

Sakharov's journey to Gorki has been a noble one. He spent a great deal of his life pampered by the very society that now represses him. He gave it all up for a fight against injustice, a fight for his own ideals of freedom and peace.

We know that the worldwide attention he focused on human rights has helped a great many dissidents, giving them at least the knowledge that people all over the world know of their suffering, and care. But, despite all of his attempts to bring change to his country's system of government and all his hopes for democracy and cooperation between the nations of the world, it seems that nothing has changed. The Soviet socialist machine continues to churn, spitting out some who do not approve of its actions and swallowing forever hundreds of others.

It seems unlikely at this time that the reforms Sakharov

has proposed will ever be enacted. Back in 1973, Jay Axelbank of *Newsweek* asked Dr. Sakharov why he continued his fight when it didn't seem to be producing any results. Sakharov told him simply that, "For us, it is not a political struggle. It is a moral struggle. We have to be true to ourselves. . . . "

AN UPDATE

In November 1985, a long-awaited meeting took place between President Ronald Reagan and Soviet leader Mikhail Gorbachev. The whole world focused on the two superpowers and their leaders, their personalities and ambitions, and their foreign and domestic policies. Each country had much to win or lose, not only in the outcome of the talks concerning arms control and other issues, but also by the way its leader was perceived in the international arena.

Two weeks before this historic summit meeting, the Soviet government made a startling announcement— Elena Bonner Sakharov, in internal exile in the city of Gorki with her renowned husband, would be allowed to leave the Soviet Union to receive medical treatment. A few days later, after the announcement, Tatyana and Efrem Yankelevich, Elena's daughter and son-in-law, were allowed to speak to Elena Bonner and Dr. Sakharov over the telephone. It was the first time they had heard Dr. Bonner's voice in over a year, Dr. Sakharov's in over five. Although the conversation was short, and certainly monitored by the KGB, it was a happy one. The rumor was confirmed—Elena would be allowed to visit Italy and the United States.

She would leave at the beginning of December, as soon as she made certain that her husband, who had recently undergone an excruciating hunger strike on her behalf, was well enough to survive a long, cold, lonely winter by himself. Dr. Bonner would travel to Italy for eye treatment, then go on to Boston to visit her family and receive treatment for her chronic heart condition. After approximately three months, she would return to her husband, and they would live out their undetermined sentence of exile in Gorki.

But there was to be a condition put on these arrangements. While out of the country, Dr. Bonner could not make any statements to the press about anything except her own medical condition. If she did talk to the press, she would not be allowed to return to the Soviet Union, ever.

As of this writing (December 16, 1985), Dr. Bonner has kept this promise she was forced to make, refusing to speak to the thousands of journalists who have surrounded her since she arrived in Italy on December 2, and in Boston a week later. But, through her children here, we have learned some disturbing details about Dr. Sakharov's latest hunger strike, which took place over a period of five months, from April to September 1985. This grueling undertaking may have been a crucial factor in Dr. Bonner's release.

A story in *The New York Times*, December 4, 1985, revealed that on April 16, 1985, Dr. Sakharov began yet another fast in an effort to obtain permission for his wife to leave the country. Six days later, he was taken to a hospital in Gorki, where he was fed by force: "His nose would be clamped shut," the *Times* reported, "and when he opened his mouth for air, food would be poured in." His wife heard nothing from him until July 11, when he turned up at their home, wearing the same outfit he was wearing when taken to the hospital. He had, it was reported, written a letter to Mikhail Gorbachev, pleading for Elena's right to travel, and had suspended his fast while awaiting a reply. When none came, he resumed his hunger strike, then was taken to the hospital again, where he remained until September 5.

Throughout the fast, Soviet authorities faked telegrams to Sakharov's friends and relatives, and produced videotapes that attempted to show Dr. Sakharov in a normal, healthy environment and condition. All the while, he was in a hospital, suffering under brutal conditions, not only from his own painful fasting, but from the indignities of force-feeding as well.

Finally, in early September, the Soviet government relented. Elena Bonner would be allowed to leave the Soviet Union, if she promised that she would not give news conferences or interviews. (They announced this to the world a few weeks later.) Dr. Sakharov stopped his fast and was allowed to return home. He is in their small apartment in Gorki now.

The story of Dr. and Mrs. Sakharov is not over. The meaning of Elena Bonner's release is at best ambiguous, and the reasons behind the decision will probably never be known. We can assume that a clue can be found in the timing—the grateful international response to the announcement of her imminent arrival warmed the climate for the Gorbachev-Reagan meeting. And Dr. Sakharov's steely will, but frail physical condition, made yet another hunger strike far too dangerous for the Soviet government to allow.

But neither does the Soviet decision end their persecution. Dr. Sakharov was secretly filmed as he accompanied his wife to the train station in Gorki. The film was released to the international media to prove that Sakharov was well. When Dr. Bonner attempted to tell him of this secret filming during a telephone call to Gorki, the phone call was jammed: static and a loud buzzing sound were heard, then the call was disconnected. The very fact that Dr. Bonner is not allowed to speak to the press while away from the Soviet Union testifies to the fear the Soviet government has of the power of freedom, the power of words, of peace.

We can be grateful that Elena Bonner will be well taken care of here, and will presumably return to the Soviet Union stronger than she left it. We know she will need that strength, for the Sakharovs, we can be sure, will continue to fight against seemingly impossible odds to have their message of peace and human rights heard throughout their country and the world.

SUGGESTED FURTHER READING

About the Soviet Union:
Klose, Kevin. *Russia and the Russians.* New York: W.W. Norton, 1983.

Kaiser, Robert G. *Russia: The People and the Power.* New York: Washington Square Press, 1976.

Shipler, David K. *Russia: Broken Idols, Solemn Dreams.* New York: Viking Penguin, 1983.

Smith, Hedrick. *The Russians.* New York: Ballantine Books, 1976.

About or by Andrei Sakharov:
Babyonyshev, Alexander, editor. *On Sakharov.* New York: Alfred A. Knopf, 1982.

Sakharov, Andrei. *Progress, Co-Existence and Intellectual Freedom.* New York: The New York Times Company, 1968.

―――.*My Country and the World.* New York: Alfred A. Knopf, 1975.

―――.*Alarm and Hope.* New York: Alfred A. Knopf, 1978.

Salisbury, Harrison. *Sakharov Speaks.* New York: Alfred A. Knopf, 1974.

INDEX

ABOUT THE AUTHOR

Suzanne LeVert is a free-lance writer and editor from Rockport, Massachusetts. She has lived in New York City since 1978 and thinks she'll remain there. Among her many projects and incarnations that come with the free-lance life, she has been project editor for the Nancy Drew, Hardy Boys, and Bobbsey Twins series, had a brief stint as a costume mistress at La MaMa Experimental Theater Company, and was Assistant Editor at *Trialogue,* the magazine of the Trilateral Commission, not necessarily in that order. Her primary interests lie in international affairs and publishing. *The Sakharov File* represents an exciting combination of both.